WALTER STEPHEN was born in Thurso, Caith[...] universities in Glasgow and Edinburgh, wit[...] History and Education. He was Principal Teacher oi ɢₑₒ₉... guished schools in Fife and Edinburgh, then became the first Adviser in Social Studies in Edinburgh and Senior Adviser in Lothian Region. In schools shrunk by falling student numbers, he set up Castlehill Urban Studies Centre, the first successful Urban Studies Centre in Britain, and the History of Education Centre.

As an independent scholar he has been active in investigating Interesting Victorians and has been responsible for books on Patrick Geddes (planner and polymath), Willie Park Junior ('The Man who took Golf to the World'), Frank Fraser Darling (born in 1903, but a Victorian in spirit who lived among the red deer and founded the environmental movement) and Charles Darwin (in *The Evolution of Evolution: Darwin, Enlightenment and Scotland*).

Contents

Illustrations – Colour Plates

Illustrations – Figures

Acknowledgements

SOMEONE LIKE THE AUTHOR, racketing round at random, depends on slight acquaintances and chance meetings to make his connections. A ranger of the US National Parks Service, J Sybenga of the Schotse Huizen in Veere, the nice man on the Elbe steamer, and many others all helped, as Pooh-Bah says in *The Mikado*, to provide 'corroborative detail, intended to give artistic verisimilitude to an otherwise bald and unconvincing narrative'.

More specifically, the staff of that great institution, the National Library of Scotland, have been helpful beyond the call of duty. The keen eye of Alice Jacobs helped to convert what might have been total confusion into an acceptable degree of randomness. Professor Bill McBride of UCLA provided opportunities which made some of the visits described possible. Wolfram Schaue showed steely determination in penetrating into parts of the *Festspielhaus* in Hellerau I could not reach. Claire Geddes put me on the trail of the elusive cuckoo. Anne-Michelle Slater of Aberdeen University acted as a mirror whose reflections refined crude early ideas.

Unless otherwise noted, the colour plates and black and white illustrations are the author's.

PLATE 2A (*Felsenlandschaft im Elbsandsteingebirge* by Caspar David Friedrich), from the Belvedere, Vienna, is reproduced by kind permission of the Österreichische Galerie Belvedere.

In regards to the following illustrations, every reasonable attempt has been made to obtain permission to reproduce the originals – FIGS 12, 13, 14, 21 and 22.

The clear and illuminating diagrams (FIGS 2–8) and sketches (FIGS 10–11) are by Olrig Stephen.

CHAPTER I

The Random Thoughts of a Random Fellow

CONSIDER THE SUMMER of 1941 in the Chilterns. Historians tell us that this saw our country at just about its lowest ebb. Catastrophe in Greece and Crete meant that nowhere in continental Europe was there a British presence. In North Africa, Rommel was poised for the invasion of Egypt. At sea, German surface raiders and U-boats were threatening to starve Britain into submission. Although the bombing of British cities had passed its peak, the possibility of its resumption was still a major disruption to civilian life.

An RAF Sergeant Instructor is based at the big RAF Training School at Halton, in Buckinghamshire. His is essentially a nine-to-five job and he has permission to sleep outside the camp, except for doing the occasional guard duty. From Scotland he brings down his wife and family – an eight-year-old boy and a little girl on the way. They have a single room, with shared kitchenette, in a big Edwardian house, set in a large garden. This is a wonderful place to spend a wonderful summer and the little boy swallows up memories like a black hole sucks in matter. Sunday is a day for walks and on this particular hot Sunday we have climbed the scarp slope of the Chilterns. Just below the lightning-struck and camouflaged monument on Coombe Hill (PLATE 1A) we have subsided on to the beautiful close turf of the hillside, had our picnic and now it is time for Father to read.

Off he goes and within minutes we are all laughing, not smiling quietly, or tittering, but laughing loud and uproariously, heads thrown back and the reader unable to continue as the tears roll down. Jerome K Jerome was demonstrating his power. Jerome K Jerome (1859–1927) had died 14 years before this little incident, yet the episode of Harris and the pie from *Three Men in a Boat* was so fresh that it could reduce a whole family to hysterics. That is power. Power at its most genial, but power nonetheless.

For us, that summer, *Three Men in a Boat* was not a modern classic, but a cheerful tale of local places we could easily reach by train or Green Line bus, or situations we might have experienced. How often have we, like the author, spent a whole day in somewhere like the British Library, combing through the medical dictionary to make the worrying discovery that we are suffering from every complaint in the book, except for Housemaid's Knee. Then we start worrying about why we are not suffering from that dire complaint.

In those distant days families like ours would still gather round the piano of an evening, with a few friends, and make our own entertainment. Thus we could appreciate another of JK Jerome's set-pieces, where the narrator is a guest at such an event. His host takes him to one side to explain that Herr Hummel, who is about to sing, is one of Germany's leading exponents of the comic song. As the song proceeds, it sounds pretty doleful, but this must be the German sense of humour. The narrator and his circle whoop with laughter and slap their thighs with enthusiasm – only to find, as we have already guessed, that the *Lieder* singer has been describing the sorrows of the shepherdess betrayed by her lover and left to perish in the mountain snows.

The memory of our little group reclining on the hillside sets me off at another tangent. As we will see, one place can set off a whole string of connections. GK Chesterton (1874–1936), if he is remembered at all, is remembered as the creator of Father Brown, the modest little priest-detective. Chesterton was a master of paradox and in his essay 'A Piece of Chalk' he starts off with a staggering one.

With enthusiasm he describes the simple pleasure of going out of London into the countryside to sketch in the open air, armed with big pieces of brown paper and coloured chalks. A couple of pages on the anticipated delights of sketching come to an abrupt halt when he discovers that he has left behind the white chalk. White chalk is of absolute importance and what follows is another couple of pages of self-reproach for forgetting this essential.

Then comes the stunning revelation that he is standing on 'a piece of chalk' – a piece of chalk which has its core in Salisbury Plain and which sends off great limbs across south and east England. The Chiltern Hills continue as the Lincolnshire and Yorkshire Wolds to Flamborough Head. The North and South Downs frame the Weald of Kent, Sussex and Hampshire. Another limb sweeps south through Dorset to the Isle of Purbeck and the Isle of Wight. For white chalk, all that Chesterton had to do was reach down and pick up any of the stones lying at his feet.

Chesterton's final big idea is to remind us of these great bands of chalk running across south-east England, of their similarity and openness, and of their long prehistory as trackways for farmers and traders in ancient times. Along the Icknield Way, one of the oldest roadways in Europe, the comparatively open chalk hills gave an easy route across England. It was used by flint traders from Norfolk before the use of metal was known in these islands, and by medieval merchants on their way to the great spring fairs in Norfolk. Chaucer's pilgrims followed the North Downs on their way to Canterbury. In our own time, the kites and gliders cavort and soar way above the Dunstable Downs in a display of freedom and energy.

And we were reclining at our ease on a piece of chalk, listening to the voice of JK Jerome, genial creator of *Three Men in a Boat: To Say Nothing of the Dog*, which has spawned at least one film and a television series featuring three contemporary humourists, which was in turn followed by further series in which the hapless trio have mishaps with boats in the waters of Britain and the Adriatic.

Jerome K Jerome is usually considered one of those 'one-book wonders', but 11 years after *Three Men in a Boat* the characters went off to Germany, the result being *Three Men on the Bummel* – like most follow-ups not a patch on its predecessor.

JK Jerome wrote nine novels, seven collections of short stories, ten sets of essays and sketches, 21 plays and seven miscellaneous works. Add to the catalogue an autobiography and six years as editor and contributor to *The Idler* magazine. Throw in service in World War 1 as an ambulance driver in the French army and one marvels at the man's industry. And yet his work reads so effortlessly!

In 1886 there had appeared *The Idle Thoughts of an Idle Fellow*, a collection of essays and sketches in the light and pleasant style he demonstrated for most of his career. This was obviously false modesty, but it gave me the title for this book. We have already seen how a little picnic on the Chilterns can lead in several directions, so where did the Random Thoughts come from?

About 12 years ago, I made a terrifying discovery. Like many another, I have always enjoyed going to new places and exploring in a very tame sort of way. For years I would look up a place and say that I would like to go there sometime. I would celebrate my retirement by taking the Maharaja Train across Rajasthan. Another time I had this mental picture of myself celebrating the same event on my balcony of the 5-star Hotel Grand Victoria Jungfrau in Interlaken, sipping my white wine as I admired the alpenglow on the face of the Jungfrau.

The discovery will not seem unusual to most. It was simply that, if one thinks in terms of annual summer holidays, there was only a finite number left to me. I was not suffering from some life-threatening illness – but I could not count on an endless succession of summer holidays.

In 1972 The Ecologist article 'Blueprint for Survival' predicted that the world's supplies of lead would give out in ten years. Ten years from 1973 took us to 1983, yet, as far as I am aware, there still seems to be enough lead to go around. Why? I know nothing of the detail, but it must be something to do with the fact that we now seem to manage quite well without putting scarce lead in our petrol.

Now we are being told that commercial fishing will wipe out fish stocks by 2048, which is very worrying. Even more worrying to me is the fact that I shall not be around in 2048 to check the accuracy of the forecast, or to see whether, by some miracle of science or uncharacteristic human self-discipline, catastrophe is avoided. I do not think I have a fear of death as such, more a certainty of oblivion, a stark terror that the world will go on birling without me and I shall know nothing of it.

My response to this appalling prospect has been to be a little more purposeful in conducting my life. Where shall we go next? became a priority. Towards the end of each year I jot down a list of things to be done or places to visit in the following year. Not necessarily big things, but things to be tidied away. For example, one day I went to Thurso with a photograph of a fat (healthy!) child on the beach, taken in 1934. On the precise spot on the vast beach where I had played I found a young mother and her two young children. Something about continuity and traditional values was very satisfying about this little episode, although I have to say the young mum looked at me a little oddly.

In the same way as The Idle Thoughts of an Idle Fellow was obviously an example of false modesty it will be clear that The Random Thoughts of a Random Fellow are not really random. They may be the purposeful tidying up of missed opportunities or the expression of one's ability to take a sideways look at matters and ask the question others seem to have missed. Or, remembering that under Elgar's *Enigma Variations* there may be another theme that has been unsuccessfully sought after for over a century, is there another, deeply embedded, thought that is anything but random? Or is it just our northern longing for the sun and colour of the south?

The Germans have a word for it. We know *Heimweh* (homesickness), but they also have *Fernweh*, which we could call farsicknesss, the longing for faraway places. The people of northern Europe have always had this longing for the south, for its warmth and colour. Goethe (1749–1832) wrote '*Kennst du das Land wo die Zitronen blühn?*' (Do you know the land where the lemon trees bloom?) expressing the melancholy ache for a faraway golden land – '*Dahin! Dahin! Möcht ich mit dir, o mein Geliebter, ziehn!*' (There, there, I would go, Oh my beloved, with thee!). Where the lemon trees bloom is along the Mediterranean coast, what we now call the French and Italian Rivieras, where Menton has the mildest winters of mainland France and every town has its Festival of Lemons in the spring.

Ambroise Thomas's *Mignon* is a 19th-century opera version of Goethe's *Wilhelm Meister* and from it '*Connais-tu le pays?*' became a great favourite for the soprano in the opera house and the salon, prostrating audiences with its affecting nostalgic simplicity. Mignon sings of dim memories of her childhood – the land from which she was abducted – and in Act III all is satisfactorily resolved. Elgar celebrated the feeling with his overture *In the South – Alassio*, and at the beginning of Thomas Mann's *Death in Venice* Aschenbach longs for the exotic south. His reluctance to leave it costs him his life.

Our own Lord Byron had his own ironic parody:

Know ye the land where the cypress and myrtle
Are emblems of deeds that are done in their clime?
Where the rage of the vulture, the love of the turtle,
Now melt into sorrow, now madden to crime!

AE Housman (1869–1936), at the much earlier age of 20, expressed my feelings much more elegantly than I can.

Now, of my threescore years and ten,
Twenty will not come again,
And take from seventy springs a score,
It only leaves me fifty more.

And since to look at things in bloom
Fifty springs are little room,
About the woodlands I will go
To see the cherry hung with snow.

But is it enough just to go there, see it, tick the box, buy the T-shirt and move on? Goethe, the first and greatest Romantic of them all, could say that no man could just look at a view for more than quarter of an hour.

Ernest Raymond (1888–1974) was a top-class old-fashioned novelist. His *A Chorus Ending* (1961) was essentially a retelling of the Crippen murder case. It began with Mr Filmer, a retired civil servant, gazing at the heights of Hampstead and reflecting on the sequent occupance of a north London suburb – on the way in which the landscape before him had changed over time. Like Goethe, Mr Filmer did not content himself with passive appreciation. He must dig to find the answers to 'Where?' and 'Why there?' He has shown himself to be a skilled observer. He then proceeded to demonstrate the skills of research and recording, ending with communication when:

> … much pleased with a scholarly piece of research, he hurried like a schoolboy to report his success to Miss Piers.

It is now fashionable to have glossily illustrated books of lists, like *The World's Best One Hundred Places*, or *The Best 100 Getaways*, or *A Thousand Things to Do Before You Die*, or even *Ten Wild Places to go for a Swim*. I find such books grossly insulting. Who is going to tell me what is best for me? What to do or what to see before I die?

Walter's Wiggles is a book about Place, organised around *Random Thoughts* – some of which might be Big Ideas. There is the importance of childhood memories and the wish to see places before it is too late. There is the craving of the northerner for the light and romance of the south. There is Goethe's notion that we should be interacting with the environment and not just staring at it. There is the concept of sequent occupance, where the image of a landscape changes with – for example – changes in technology.

Come with me round some of my 'random' places and see why I think they are important. What do they tell us about ourselves? Come and join me as I go from one to the other. Few of them are World Heritage sites. Most of them are off the beaten track – although not very far. I think I can guarantee an interesting journey.

One last thought but not a random one. Elgar's *Enigma Variations* are 16 musical portraits of his friends, identified by their initials or nicknames. The best known is *Nimrod*, heard on great state occasions. *Nimrod* ('a mighty hunter before the Lord') was an affectionate portrait of Edward Jaeger, whose family introduced healthy woollen underwear to Britain, and who published Elgar's music. (*Jäger* is a hunter in German – a neat little pun.) The relationship between each variation and the basic theme is clear enough, but some scholars believe that there may be another theme, deeply embedded, that has been unsuccessfully sought after for over a century.

In the same way, readers of this book may think the arrangement of chapters is random. But as one reads on it may appear that there is some order. The early chapters have a touch of Romanticism, of Man in awe at the forces of Nature, of beauty all around us. But as the book proceeds, the mood darkens as we observe how many people misbehave and misuse this wonderful world. We are left with the question as to what kind of world we want to leave to the next generation.

CHAPTER 2

The Cradle of the Sublime

WE ARE LOOKING at a picture of *Chalk Cliffs on Rügen*, an island in the Baltic. Framed by a tree, the sea is grey-blue and the cliffs are startlingly white. Beneath us and to the right is a small dark figure with folded arms looking out to sea. The lonely figure is lost in contemplation of the silent scene and because we are looking over his shoulder we cease to be spectators and begin to identify with the deep sense of solitude of this mysterious watcher. The spectator of the picture thinks himself in the watcher's place, to become conscious of his own inadequacy and how tiny he is before the infinity of nature.

Caspar David Friedrich (1774–1840) was born across the bay from Rügen and frequently returned there. He worked in Copenhagen and Berlin before settling in Dresden as Associate Professor at the Academy in 1815. He grew up and lived with the influences of Goethe, Schiller and Kant. He read ETA Hoffmann and knew Schubert's songs. He made many trips into the Riesengebirge south of Dresden and in July 1813, after the French had entered Dresden, he retired into voluntary exile in the *Elbsandsteingebirge*.

There he painted *The Graves of Fallen Freedom Fighters*. Two French chasseurs, their backs turned towards us, are keeping watch close to a sarcophagus in a wild, rocky landscape. The soldiers are small, the monument unnaturally bright. A recent drama by Kleist (*Hermannschlacht*) had retold the story of Arminius, who had defeated the might of Rome. Friedrich's picture caught the moment and was first shown in an exhibition of patriotic art organised after Dresden had been recaptured by the Russians under Prince Repain.

The symbolism of the picture is unequivocal. The foreign soldiers are guarding the tomb of Christ and there will be a secular resurrection resulting in the expulsion of the French and the liberation of Germany, as Hermann had disposed of Varus's legions in 9AD.

On several counts Friedrich is clearly a Romantic. He advocates the rights of indigenous populations to throw off foreign rule and work out their own destinies. His stance as the lone observer is that of the free spirit confronting the great mysteries of life and coming up with his own solutions. Although from the 1820s there were to be no more patriotic works. Professor Boyd White of Edinburgh, the expert on Friedrich, tells us that:

> ... the wanderer seems to be aware of his own inadequacy: he is essentially a spectator.
>
> ... Vicariously we become the wanderer and experience the smallness of man before the infinity of nature... the individual's deep sense of solitude and quest for a harmonious union with God.

By contrast, another, more simply representational, almost photographic, aspect of Romanticism – Man in the Mountains – was initiated on 24 January 1801, when Hans Conrad Escher von der Linth (1767–1823) published the first *Panorama of the Alps*, the view from the top of the Niederhorn, near Interlaken.

Friedrich's Romanticism is lower key and more subtle. In his winter landscapes we see the pine forest, with wisps of mist. Concentrating hard, we see in the forest a tall crucifix, sometimes with unnatural light from some unknown source. Or a fragile, slender, almost ghostly, Gothic church stands half-hidden in the fir trees. Or again, we see a prehistoric megalith on a snowy knoll, guarded by three ancient shattered pines. The evergreen fir tree is, of course, a symbol of Christian hope and one implication is that God is to be found more easily in the quiet of the forest or the mountain than in the royal court.

The judicious use of violet and other dark colours created a mood of melancholy and resignation. However, it has to be admitted that, for example, his *Fishing Boat by the Baltic Sea* of c.1830–1835 in the Thyssen-Bornemisza Museum of Madrid is so dark as to be almost meaningless, unless it is that there is a glimpse of light at the end of the darkest tunnel.

A walk round the Gemäldegalerie Neue Meister in Dresden reveals that stillness is a characteristic of Friedrich's work. This seems an odd word to use; after all, until the invention of cinematography every painting, sketch or engraving was a still picture. But generations of artists have become expert at depicting or suggesting movement or action. Think of Turner's snowstorm with a ship at sea, or the agonies of Géricault's *Raft of the Medusa,* or Brueghel's *Massacre of the Innocents,* all alive with electric tension.

Boyd White suggests that Friedrich's feelings had moved from a direct link with Christianity to a looser:

> consideration of natural phenomena as a manifestation of the Absolute, a pantheistic belief that held that each natural phenomenon is endowed with a soul.

Criticism of his work became harsher. His landscapes began to be felt monotonous, gloomy and old-fashioned. Increasingly he felt isolated and misunderstood. From 1824 Friedrich's health began to deteriorate. He had a stroke on 26 June 1825. Another in 1835 finished him as a creator and he died on 7 May 1840.

Today's visitor to the gallery is unlikely to react in the same way as Friedrich's silent watcher on the *Chalk Cliffs on Rügen.* But if he pauses at all he is likely to wonder at the countless skeletons and shells of tiny creatures which have been collected, compressed and uplifted over an immensity of time and at the solidity and uniformity of the chalk which they became. Where do I fit into this? he asks himself. What will become of me? What is it all for?

Friedrich still has the power to disturb, which makes him a Great Romantic. For example, when the Scottish Chamber Orchestra had a series of concerts under the rubric Great Romantics, each concert with a Weber overture, a Mendelssohn concerto and a Schumann symphony, it was Friedrich's *Moonrise on the Seashore* (1822) that was overprinted for the programme.

CHAPTER 3

The Wolf's Glen

DRESDEN WAS ONE of my first targets when I set out to tidy up my life. It kept on bobbing up in so many connections. It had been a beautiful city. It had been devastated by bombing. There were the crossed swords of Meissen pottery, with its Dresden shepherdesses. Time and again familiar names were linked with the city. Surely it was necessary to go there and work out for myself how much of the city's reputation was myth and how much hard fact. As it turned out, more than one visit was required to get at the truth about Dresden.

In 1979 I travelled by train from Berlin to Prague. In those days of the German Democratic Republic, Dresden was the last stop before entering Czechoslovakia and we sat in the station for two hours cooling our heels as frontier-crossers and police came and went. Approaching and leaving the city it was clear that there were still great swathes of blackened ruins left from that terrible night in February 1945. As, eventually, we clanked towards the border, I brooded on the sufferings of the poor people, the damage to lives and property and the fact that – after more than 30 years – there was so much still to be done to restore the city to something approaching normality.

For years I continued to brood. Why was there so much fuss about Dresden when, for example, Hamburg's fire storm had destroyed more of the city and killed more of its people? The answer seemed to lie in our perception of these places. If anything, Hamburg was the place where The Beatles learned their trade in the red light district of the Reeperbahn. But Dresden seemed to be something special, a city of culture whose destruction had an extra dimension of vandalism. Dresden was the home of great art, of great buildings, of famous names.

Increasingly I felt the need to go and see for myself. Was it all myth and propaganda? Or was there something special about Dresden that made its destruction a greater crime – if it was a crime – than the destruction of Hamburg or a dozen industrial towns in the Ruhr?

And so to Carl Maria von Weber – a Romantic name for a Romantic composer. His birth was also suitably Romantic. The son of a consumptive mother, a congenital hip disease gave him a limp for life – like Byron, the supreme Romantic, who died while taking part in the Greek struggle for independence. Weber was born on 18 November 1786 in Eutin, near Lübeck on the Baltic Sea. The area was known as 'the Switzerland of Holstein' – another element in his Romantic start!

He grew up in a Romantic atmosphere to become one of the most progressive composers of the early 19th century and a great virtuoso pianist – his father recognised his genius early and promoted him as another young Mozart. Often we hear in the duller patches of Weber's music a taste of Wagner (1813–1883), only to remember that Weber was from the generation before that of the great rebel. Weber served in Dresden from 1817 till 1825, while Wagner fled from that city in 1848, the Year of Revolutions.

In *Enchanted Wanderer: The Life of Carl Maria von Weber* (2007) Lucy and Richard Stebbins reproduce a contemporary painting which shows a handsome young man with Romantic curls, a long face and dark eyes, thoughtfully leaning against a pedestal. A drawing of 1825, later in the book, is less flattering. In profile the composer is reading the score of *Euryanthe* with the aid of a magnifying glass. He has glasses and an exceedingly aquiline nose, hollow cheeks and a mop of tight curls.

Carl Maria grew up in a hothouse of musical talent. His father was a professional musician of some distinction. Genoveva, his mother, was a brilliant singer who was later to be buried in the Mozart family grave in Salzburg. His uncle had four lively, good-looking and warm-hearted daughters. They were also extremely talented – we know this from the music specially written for them by the greatest composers of the day. Constanze married Mozart while Aloysia, whom Mozart probably should have married, still lives through the pyrotechnic *Exultate Jubilate* he wrote for her.

Weber's life was the treadmill of the Romantic artist, desperately trying to stay alive with reluctant patrons and an insensitive public. In the index to the Stebbins' book under 'Weber: Wanderings' they list 59 towns, all German-speaking except for Paris, Copenhagen, Prague and London, with nothing faster than a galloping horse to connect them!

Weber died a suitably Romantic death of consumption (tuberculosis) and self-sacrifice in London on 5 June 1826, in his 40th year. He knew he was very gravely ill and that travel would almost certainly finish him off, but he had a wife and family and there was money to be made in the British capital. To the critic Böttiger he said:

> It's all one! Whether I go or not, in a year I'm a dead man. But if I go, my children will eat when their father's dead, and if I stay they'll starve. What would you do in my place?

On 16 February he left Dresden and fewer than four months later he was dead. But in that time his opera *Oberon* had been premiered and given a string of performances. There was a series of concerts and personal appearances and he even had the generosity to give a free concert for charity.

Although not in the top flight of the great composers, Weber left us a stream of beautiful music, brilliant, sometimes sweetly sentimental, and occasionally disturbingly dark. The premiere of *Der Freischütz* at the brand-new Schauspielhaus in Berlin on 18 June 1821, is generally regarded as the foundation of the German operatic tradition and he influenced many German composers into the 20th century. (Sadly, the premiere was something of a disappointment for him. His opera was to have been the first work performed in the new theatre but at the last minute a new drama by Goethe stole his thunder.)

Central to the Romantic Movement was Sir Walter Scott, himself influenced by Goethe, although they never met. Although Scott made it a rule 'seldom to read and never to answer foreign letters from literary folks', for him 'Goethe is different and a wonderful fellow'. In his *Journal* on 15 February 1827 Scott rather naively and modestly marvels;

> Who could have told me 30 years ago I should correspond and on something like an equal footing with the Author of *The Robbers*?

(which Scott thought he had translated in 1799).[1]

Enthusiasm for the Waverley Novels swept across Europe and, in Germany especially, gallant chivalry and romantic nationalism found devoted followers. Sir Walter Scott's *Minstrelsy of the Scottish Border* of 1802 was discovered by Achim von Arnim, who, with Clemens Brentano, 'practically founded the German Romantic delight in the Rhein with their journey along it to collect their folk-songs, guitars slung over their shoulders'. In 1805 their collection of folk songs, *Des Knaben Wunderhorn*, was published, to be mined by later Romantics, most famously the composer Gustav Mahler. In 1812–1815 the *Kinder-* and

Hausmärchen – definitely not fairy tales – of the Brothers Grimm appeared. The high point of Romanticism was the Tale of Terror – the *Schauerroman* – and, at the same time as the collectors were picking the brains of the peasants, ETA Hoffmann's strange imagination provided the spark for a dozen operas, ballets and the novel of suspense.

It was Edmund Burke in *On the Sublime and Beautiful* (1756) who had made it clear that Romanticism was not only to be the pursuit of 'the beautiful ideal' but was to touch the sublime through 'grief, danger, the menacing power of nature.'

Der Freischütz (1821) was a Tale of Terror set to music. It tells the story of the marksman who enlists the powers of evil to make magical bullets and is only one strand of such tales prevalent in Central Europe. There the vast game-filled forests have been the source of an endless, rich folklore for Germans similar to that of the shore-dwelling Celts of northern Europe and the sea – the friend-enemy, provider-destroyer, mother-betrayer.

Weber arrived in Dresden on 13 January 1817, taking up the post of Musikdirektor to the King of Saxony. He was based there until he left on his last journey in February 1826. In a typically Romantic muddle the chain of command at the Saxon court was unclear. He had thought he had been invited to be Kapellmeister, only to be told that he was nothing more than 'Music Director of the German Opera' – a situation ripe for exploitation by disaffected members of the court orchestra. In winter he and his family lived in the city but in summer they lived at Hosterwitz, upstream of Dresden, and convenient for the royal castle at Pillnitz where the king spent his summers. The Webers were too poor to furnish two houses, so their furniture was moved to and from Dresden every autumn and spring. The Weber circle loved Hosterwitz and it became very popular. Picturesquely set, it had fine views and dramatic walks in the nearby 'Saxon Switzerland'. It was here that the strands of the Romantic movement became intertwined.

Meanwhile, back in Edinburgh George Thomson had for half a century been Secretary to the Board for the Encouragement of Arts and Manufactures in Scotland. In touch with all parts of the country, he was a formidable collector of the folk songs of his native Scotland, Ireland and Wales. It was for Thomson that Burns rewrote the words or wrote new and lovely poems to the 'auld Scots sangs'. Thomson engaged the leading composers of the time, Haydn and Beethoven, to write accompaniments and arrangements for these traditional airs. In 1825 Weber was also commissioned by Thomson to contribute arrangements for flute, violin, cello and piano. Proud to be a successor of Haydn in this great enterprise, Weber set 12 of the songs 'clearly and with charm.' Sadly, he never saw the finished work, as he died before the set could be published.

Thomson was clearly following up on the success of *Der Freischütz*, which still holds a regular place in the operatic repertoire, particularly in the German-speaking countries. A tale of unrequited love, jealousy and dealing with the Devil would seem to be totally irrelevant to sophisticates of today. How can selling one's soul to the Devil worry someone who doesn't believe in 'the prince of darkness'? The stage settings, with mysterious forests, misty glens, bats, owls and ghostly apparitions might seem to be corny – a kind of Teutonic Brigadoon – but once the action gets moving, the music takes over and disbelief is suspended.

Weber's choruses caught the mood of the moment, with music whose earthy tunefulness came directly from German folk-song, matching patriotic sentiments with recognisably national sounds. The women sing with lyrical beauty yet, particularly in the scene in the Wolf's Glen, Weber contrives to chill the spine as the powers of darkness supervise the casting of the magical bullets.

When he came to compose the music for *Der Freischütz* Weber himself said –

> I had to remind the hearer of these 'dark powers' by means of tone-colour and melody as often as possible... I gave a great deal of thought to the question of what was the right principal colouring for this sinister element. Naturally it had to be a dark, gloomy colour... particularly the lowest register of the clarinet, which seemed especially suitable for depicting the sinister... *this* gives the opera its principal character.

Caspar David Friedrich did the poster for the Berlin premiere. It shows the Wolf's Glen as a maelstrom of rocks, trees and mist – with more than a passing resemblance to several of his landscapes. Is it just a coincidence that the villain of the opera is Caspar?

In far-off Edinburgh the first performance of *Der Freischütz* took place on 29 December 1824. Miss Stephens, a leading soprano of the time was 'quite delightful'. The young Charles Darwin, writing to his father on 23 October 1825, said: 'On Monday we are going to Der Fr. (I do not know how to spell the rest of the word).'

The mature Darwin was a rational observer and recorder. Could it be that, underneath, there was a touch of the Romantic? We do not know how he reacted to the Wolf's Glen and the Satanic casting of magical bullets, but in *The Voyage of the Beagle* there are at least two moments capable of a Romantic interpretation. Twice in the Chilean Andes he objectively describes and explains the geology and (in one case) the forests of Chilean sugar palm, before moving on to subjective enjoyment of the night on La Campana, in one case, and when: 'The mind seemed to grow giddy by looking so far into the abyss of time.'[2] A mental picture comes to mind of Darwin as one of Caspar David Friedrich's silent watchers.

The relationship between Weber and his favourite instrument is absorbing. Weber was fortunate in that his arrival in Munich in 1811 brought him into contact with Heinrich Bärmann, the most distinguished clarinettist of the day. The clarinet had just become technically mature. Haydn used it at the end of his career and Mozart established it in the orchestra. A school of virtuosos appeared and a maturely German Romantic use of clarinet evolved. The German style was soft, rich and full in tone, in contrast to the shriller and more brilliant French manner. With Bärmann's new ten-key clarinet Weber – according to the Stebbinses –

> found an instrument that with its French incisiveness and vivacity and its German fullness seemed to express a new world of feeling, and to match both the dark romantic melancholy and the extrovert brilliance of his own temperament.

For a concert in April 1811, Weber wrote a Concertino for Bärmann. The King of Bavaria was so impressed that he immediately ordered two clarinet concertos. Amid a flood of other compositions they were first performed in June and November of that year. With the *Grand Duo Concertante* (1816) and the *Clarinet Quintet* (1811–1815) Weber had single-handedly established a repertoire of mysterious darkness and pyrotechnic brilliance for the clarinet.

The Elbsandsteingebirge, in English, Saxon Switzerland, is now a national park 50km south of Dresden, on the Elbe near the Czech border.

The Victorians loved these far-fetched comparisons. Stockholm was the Venice of the North, Rothesay the Madeira of the Clyde and Inveresk the Montpelier of Scotland. Saxon Switzerland is not really very like Switzerland – but it is much more mountainous than the Switzerland of Holstein, where Weber had been born. As the name implies, the *Elbsandsteingebirge* is on the Elbe and is made of sandstone – not unlike the Millstone Grit of the Pennines where Heathcliff rampaged Romantically. What makes it special is not the height – only about 300 metres (1000 feet) above the river – but the fantastic array of sandstone pinnacles, cliffs and valleys accessible from the river.

For Romantics this area is a must. So on my 70th birthday I found myself getting down to the Elbe in order to get the river steamer at 9am. There was quite a queue and a group of six old wifies persisted in buying individual tickets and haggling over the change. Fortunately, a group of six young men was more sensible. One bought all the tickets and they squared up later! I was just able to step on the boat at nine, as the Frauenkirche bell was striking, and the boat set off with typical German punctuality.

The Elbe steamers are the oldest steamship line in the world and some of them are over 130 years old. This one, the *Countess Coseli*, is very modern and has at least three levels of deck. Like everything else on this day, the name was significant. Augustus the Strong, Elector of Saxony and King of Poland was immensely wealthy, a great patron of the arts and father of the aesthetic greatness of Dresden – as well as having an illegitimate child for every day of the year. Hence the nickname. (He also had one legitimate child.)

One of his mistresses, the Countess Coseli, was the prime favourite for several years, being quite strong-minded herself till she fell out of favour and was exiled to Prussia. She was brought back in exchange for some Prussian soldiers and imprisoned in 'a melancholy castle' at Steulpen, where she died after 50 years of captivity. Not for nothing was Augustus known as Strong! The Random Fellow does not have to be objective and gets quite irate at the unfairness, whereby a rich megalomaniac can treat someone he has fallen out with – who presumably had many fine qualities – like dirt. Her memory survives, however, in the splendid steamer that bears her name and serves the splendid river she knew.

There is nothing more enjoyable than a cruise on one of Europe's great rivers, especially on the top deck, with the sun shining all day. The landscape on either side changes continually as we steadily follow the bends of the river. Every now and then we stop to drop people off and to take on new passengers, many of them archetypal German nature lovers in their natural habitat and their summer plumage of sticks, rucksacks, lederhosen and feathered hats. As a great highway the Elbe serves medieval towns and picture-postcard castles.

One of these – Schloss Pillnitz – was the summer palace of Augustus the Strong, Weber's summer workplace and the Countess Coseli's home till she was disgraced. On the steamer were postcards of the 'Flood of the Century' the previous year, with the castle almost totally under water. Incredibly, from the river there is no sign of damage whatsoever; the gardens are restored and all seems normal a mere ten months since the great disaster.

This is perhaps where we should remind ourselves that the Elbe is one of the great rivers of Europe and has its place in the Romantic music of the concert hall. Smetana, the Czech composer, wrote a series of orchestral pictures called *Má Vlast* (My Country). The best-known of these portrays the twinkling ripple of a little stream which burbles on and keeps growing until it becomes a great flowing river. The piece is often called the 'Vltava', which is the Czech name of the river when it flows through Prague, but when it flows into Germany it merges into the even greater Elbe.

On we go, with people fishing on either bank and dozens of cyclists waving to us as we pass. Eventually the valley sides grow closer and rocky cliffs come into sight. This is 'Saxon Switzerland'. I disembark – with many others – at Kurort (spa) Rathen and take a side valley towards the Bastei (bastion or fortress).

Only here can one guess at the full horror of the floods of the previous year and the resilience of the Saxons. All around are green slopes with patches of woodland and wooden farmhouses covered in pretty flowers. Then one turns to climb through a little hamlet to note a metal plaque about five metres above the ground. This was the flood limit and everything below this was under river water last September. What a people – after wartime devastation and half a century of Communist misrule the Flood of the Century is suffered and repaired in double quick time!

Up in the Bastei it is easy to see where Friedrich and Weber got the Wolf's Glen from. This is a real fantasy land of cliffs and pinnacles and deep clefts with foaming waterfalls. (PLATE 1B) Great masses of bare rock are all around, yet every flat top and narrow valley is covered in pines. On one summit are the remains of a hill-fort, reminding us of the Romantic times of the heroic Hermann, when Varus's three Roman legions disappeared into the German forests without trace.

One can walk around at different levels, through the gorges and on the cliffs, looking down on the Elbe and south towards the Czech Republic. We can work out where Friedrich must have stood to make his sketches for *The Wanderer Before the Sea of Fog* (1818), or his *Bohemian Landscape* (1809) with its twin volcanic cones rising above the Elbe plain. Here he found the peace and harmony which became *The Large Enclosure near Dresden* (1832).

Two things were lacking to make this a truly Romantic experience: solitude and appropriate weather. This is a popular area, has been a popular area for many years and is also difficult – even dangerous – to walk through. Therefore there are paths and steps. In the nineteenth century massive walls and bridges were constructed and memorial plaques built in. Fortunately, local stone was used and the result is attractive access to some difficult spots. In recent years, light metal structures have made it possible to gain some of the more spectacular viewpoints safely, while the sheer quality of design has meant that they are not intrusive. (PLATE 1B)

But there are visitors, very many visitors. Some are young and fit. Others have come here for the last time. Everyone seems to be relaxed and happy among the paths and wheelchairs and snapping cameras. Beyond, the most spectacular stretch can be accessed by a circuitous road and this serves cafes, restaurants and shops – fortunately, all in character. The tour buses come here and there is an open-air theatre. It is wonderful to see so many enjoying the wonders of nature and the clean fresh air – but where is the solitude? Where can the Silent Watcher find a stance?

When Friedrich and Weber were here part of the experience was the stillness, broken only by the sounds of nature, the birds, the rushing streams, the wind in the trees. Here they were in the presence of the Sublime and could feel their imaginations stirring with Romantic notions. (PLATE 2A) Today it is interesting and beautiful and enjoyable – but impossible to be alone.

I was there on a beautiful sunny day in July, which was wrong. Everything was just too tidy. In Friedrich's forests there is a tangle of dead branches and fallen trees. In the National Park such debris is tidied away. The Romantic landscape is one of mist and mystery, with the silence enlivened by the flash of lightning and the roll of thunder. How can one feel terror when a warden will be along any minute to check that everything is *in Ordnung*? If we compare PLATES 1B and 2A, which is the more Romantic? In which can we more easily imagine the casting of magical bullets as the thunder rolls and the lightning flashes?

Nevertheless, this was a really splendid day. At its end I found my way back down to the Elbe, which was crossed by a most ingenious ferry driven by the current of the river. It has no engine but is attached to a steel cable over the river, across which it is pushed by an angled plate like a large rudder.

Romanticism is a serious business. The suicide of Goethe's Young Werther was followed by an epidemic of lovesick young men taking their own lives. After ten minutes of non-stop vocal pyrotechnics the death by consumption of Violetta brings *La Traviata* to a close. Yet the line between high drama and anticlimax is a narrow one. In my young days a music hall artist called – as I recall – Billy Dainty, made a decent living dressed as a ballet dancer and being not quite able to dance like Margot Fonteyn.

Personally I find it difficult to live a life of high seriousness all the time and therefore propose to wrap up these random thoughts by quoting from Paul Griffiths in *How to be Tremendously Tuned in to Opera*:

Carl Maria Friedrich Ernst von Weber
Led a life of most tremendous labour
Trying to write an opera not too tragical
But noble, German, and distinctly magical.
Der Freischütz filled the bill; although it's grisly,
It mixes horror with a whiff of Bisley.
You can't translate the title, but, for fun
I think of it as *Aennchen Get Your Gun*.

My patroness on this excursion had been my mother-in-law, who gave me it as a birthday present. A people-person rather than a place-person, for her the highlight of the day, repeated ad infinitum with much laughter, cut me down to size.

After about an hour on the river steamer, a German gentleman sidled up to me quietly and told me that *eine Möwe* had made a mess on my shirt and I should go downstairs and get it cleaned while it was still fresh! Luckily, I knew that a *Möwe* was a seagull, did what he suggested and reappeared – to the amusement of all – in a wet, but clean shirt. By the time we reached Rathen the breeze and sun had done their work and my new friend was able to congratulate me on my fresh appearance.

Notes

[1] Sir Walter was the most genial of men, yet he could have rather a grumpy attitude towards what we would call 'fan mail'. In his time it was the recipient who paid the cost of postage – and Scott could be:

> Annoyed beyond measure with the idle intrusion of voluntary correspondents, each man who has a pen, ink, sheet of foolscap and an hour to spare flies a letter at me. I believe the postage costs me £100. (*Journal, 6 January 1828*)

Scott wrote at a furious pace, often showed signs of tired writing and made many mistakes, despite his vast scholarship. (He frequently gave his address as 93 Castle Street when it was 39).

After 30 years Scott could be forgiven for forgetting that Schiller wrote *The Robbers* (first performed 1782) while Goethe wrote *Götz von Berlichingen* in 1773, and which Scott did translate. Online, it is described as 'the first recorded instance of a phrase now in common use as *'Leck mich am Arsch'* (literally 'lick me on my arse', ie 'kiss my arse') and euphemistically called the *Götz quote*.' I do not know how the respectable Scott got round this problem. The less respectable Mozart wrote two canons in 1782, *Leck mich em Arsch* and *Leck mir den Arsch fein recht schön sauber*.

Perhaps Scott's error was Freudian!

[2] This striking phrase of John Playfair's is examined more closely in 'The Mind Grows Giddy', the next Random Thought.

CHAPTER 4

The Mind Grows Giddy

IT WAS PROBABLY a mistake to think that one could spend three weeks with pleasure in Houston in September. Houston is a huge, prosperous city growing at an unbelievable pace. Work is everything, so there is little opportunity for moss-gathering or watching the clouds go by. Gray Line, the main tour provider in American cities, offers only two half-day tours. The NASA Headquarters tour suffers because all the real action takes place in Florida and most of the Houston activity is top secret. The city tour turns out to be an assessment of property values as we cruise past the MD Anderson Institute, the world's leading cancer centre, River Oaks, the luxury suburb where the Shah of Persia built a palace conveniently near the MD Anderson, where he died, and the municipality which has a ridiculously low speed limit and whose main source of income is fining careless motorists who unwarily drive through its territory.

In this, the hurricane season, on a Monday, it began to rain at lunchtime and just kept on raining till the trip out to the airport on Wednesday morning took on the characteristics of a wartime Combined Operation.

The highlight of Tuesday was to observe the ladies of Houston's upper crust emerging from their monthly Art Appreciation class, muttering 'Aw, Hell', stripping off their pumps and stockings and running barefoot to their limos. As the sole visitor to the fine Science Museum I was discomfited to be followed around by a huge guard 'packing a piece' as they say – a large revolver which looked as if it could blow away an enraged elephant.

Entertainment over for the day, there was no alternative but to head for the biggest bookshop in town. Being in an oil town there was a big section on geology and there I rustled about contentedly for a while. I was stunned to find a replica reprint of James Hutton's *The Theory of the Earth*, first published in 1788. Bound in with it was Playfair's 1805 *Biographical Account of the late Dr James Hutton*.

From this throbbing city devoted to the future I was transported back to the Berwickshire coast, to the day when John Playfair, Hutton and Sir James Hall sailed from Dunglass round to Siccar Point. FIG 1 is a modern sketch from the Siccar Point interpretation board, showing these three gallant representatives of the Scottish Enlightenment searching the shore, with Hutton in the stern guiding the search.

John Playfair's monument on Calton Hill is one of those which gave Edinburgh its title of 'Athens of the North'. As Professor of Natural Philosophy Playfair (1748–1819) was:

> cast in nature's happiest mould, acute, clear, comprehensive, and having all the higher qualities of intellect combined and regulated by the most perfect good taste, being not less perfect in his moral than in his intellectual nature. He was a man every way distinguished, respected, and beloved.

Sir James Hall was the first to demonstrate how limestone was metamorphosed into marble, while Hutton (1726–1797) was a doctor who had

FIG. 1
'Three men in a boat'
– off Siccar Point,
1788 style.

studied agriculture and taken up the practical applications of chemistry, moving into geology in 1768.

In Playfair's words:

> On landing at this point, we found that we actually trode on the primeval rock.
> Dr Hutton was highly pleased with appearances that set in so clear a light the different foundations of the parts which compose the exterior crust of the earth

and proceeded to interpret the 'palpable evidence' that lay before them.

What was the palpable evidence that changed people's view of the past forever? Using the modern vocabulary, in Silurian times shales and other rocks were laid down under water. This must have taken a long time.

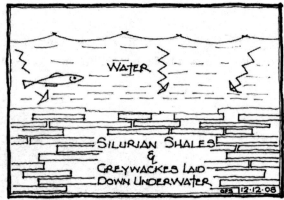

FIG. 2
Siccar Point – Phase 1.

These rocks were then tilted, uplifted and partially worn away by wind and water. This also would have taken a long time.

FIG. 3
Siccar Point – Phase 2.

In the Old Red Sandstone period the Silurian rocks were covered by water and more sediments were laid down. These included sandstones and a rock like sandstone which contained fragments from the Silurian rocks. Again, this process must have taken a long time.

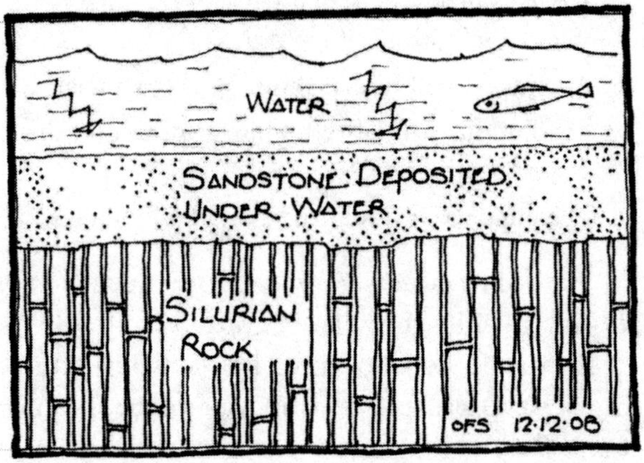

FIG. 4
Siccar Point – Phase 3.

The line separating the Silurian rocks from the newer sediments above is called an unconformity and represents a period of uplift and erosion, then submergence and deposition. In short, a very long time.

The Old Red Sandstone was horizontal and under water when its sediments were accumulating. Now it is slightly tilted and above sea level. This tilting and uplift must also have taken a long time.

FIG. 5
Siccar Point – Phase 4.

Playfair was clearly moved by the processes being revealed to him so clearly.

We often said to ourselves, what clearer evidence could we have had of the different formation of these rocks, and of the long interval which separated their formation; had we actually seen them emerging from the bosom of the deep?

We felt ourselves carried back to the time when the schistus was still at the bottom of the sea...

An epocha still more remote presented itself...

Revolutions still more remote appeared in the distance of this extraordinary perspective.

The mind seemed to grow giddy by looking so far into the abyss of time.

His conclusion was that: 'How much further reason may sometimes go than imagination can venture to follow'.

Although the whole area has similar features, the classic unconformity shown on PLATE 2B takes up little more volume than a decent sized living room. But, as Playfair further wrote:

We were truly fortunate in the course we had pursued in this excursion; a great number of other curious and important facts presented themselves and we returned, having collected, in one day, more ample materials for future speculation than have sometimes resulted from years of diligent and laborious research.

Hutton, of course, was not alone, nor the first, in his speculation about the very fundamental origins of the planet. For him 'the present was the key to the past' – there was no need for a supernatural explanation. There was 'no sign of a beginning and no sign of an end' – an uncomfortable thought which some have not had the courage to accept. Famously, or infamously, Bishop James Ussher in 1650 was able to use the Old Testament to say that the world was created on 22 October 4004BC, a Saturday, at about six in the evening. The moment of creation was so precise because the first full day would have had to be a Sunday, 'when the evening and the morning were the first day.' The Jews kept in step, estimating that the same event took place in 3761BC. For the Muslims the act of creation was of a similar order of magnitude. These dubious authorities were to prove a major obstacle to a rational understanding of natural processes.

In France, Buffon (1707–88), author of the 36-volume *Histoire Naturelle*, was another who was worrying away about the age of the

earth and the act of creation. Among much else he studied sedimentation and decided that *'chaque feuillet d'une ardoise correspond a une
marée'* (each leaf of a tile – each layer – corresponds with a former sea).
He was thus able to calculate: *'qu'une colline de mille toises de hauteur
correspond a 14,000 ans de sedimentation.'* (A hill 2,000 metres in
height therefore corresponded to 14,000 years of sedimentation.) A
toise was about two metres, the French equivalent of a fathom, therefore
– assuming the Alps were composed of uniformly uplifted sediments (in
itself a pretty big assumption) – the highest mountains of France were
about 28,000 years old. The earth was getting older, but there was still
a long way to go before Hutton introduced the concept of deep time.

I knew all this, of course, but there, in the bookshop, it struck me
that my knowledge was just book learning and I felt a craving to get
back to Berwickshire. This was not homesickness but a desire to see for
myself and to see whether I too could find something of what the three
gallant representatives of the Scottish Enlightenment had experienced.

I had been within a mile of Siccar Point many times, since it is just
off the A1, beyond Cockburnspath. As a tourist attraction, Hutton's
Unconformity rates very low. Nobody today has the necessary courage
or skill for the approach by sea. Instead there is the occasional sign
along a minor road till, near a vegetable processing plant, there is a farm
track, with a farm gate and, beside it, a perfectly decent interpretation
board. From here one crosses or goes round two fields, skirting the
clifftops till one looks down to Siccar Point, before descending a wet
slope, as steep as a grassy slope can be without becoming rocky. Great
sheets of rough Old Red Sandstone conglomerate are worked over by
the North Sea at high tide but, when the tide recedes, a complex pattern
of clefts and rock pools is revealed.

The random traveller can range all over this area looking for a fresh
view of a very familiar image, always returning to Hutton's Unconformity, the classic unconformity shown on PLATE 2B. What strikes the
modern observer is the small scale of the piece of evidence on which
Hutton built the theory which shook – and still shakes – the world.

It is lonely down here. There may be the occasional fishing boat
offshore but for living companions there are only the shags drying off
on the rocks and a few busy waders. Otherwise it is just oneself and the
rocks – and one's thoughts. As with Caspar David Friedrich's lone

observer, all is stillness and contemplation. One can see the same as Hutton did and retrace his line of reasoning. It is easy to step into the shoes of the three earnest philosophers and like them 'to grow giddy by looking so far into the abyss of time'.

It would be reasonable to expect that Hutton's 'Eureka moment' should be commemorated in some suitable way. After all, there are countless memorials to faith in the power of God – great cathedrals and temples, paintings and sculptures, places of pilgrimage, miraculous cures.

Surely here, on this lonely shore, there should be a shrine, a place of pilgrimage, dedicated to the triumph of rational thought.

However, it does not worry me that there is not a monument at Siccar Point, with the 'Go Giddy with Hutton Experience' and the 'I saw the Unconformity' T-shirt. At Tautavel in Roussillon, the earliest known site of human occupation in Europe, there is a superb interpretative complex from which one can view the excavation site through a high-powered telescope – without trampling all over it. Edinburgh has its Dynamic Earth, another superb interpretation centre using all the modern techniques to recreate the processes Hutton first described and interpreted. In Greyfriars Kirkyard there is a memorial plaque to the 'Founder of Modern Geology' while, between a multi-storey car park and some shabby tenements, the Hutton Memorial Garden marks the site of his house, where *Theory of the Earth* was written. A lump of Triassic sandstone has a cartoon of Hutton and the quotation: 'We find no vestige of a beginning, no prospect of an end'. Around are boulders from Glen Tilt and other localities associated with Hutton. Looming over the site are Salisbury Crags, with Hutton's Section and Hutton's Rock out of sight beyond the Cat's Nick, reminding us that 'humans and their petty doings come and go, but the geology endures'.

All of these, each in its own way, tells us something about Hutton and how he changed the way we think about the Earth, its age and origins.

All over the world are geological exposures – in cliffs and quarries and road cuttings, in the walls of houses and gardens – which can tell a story if we only apply the kind of thinking that Hutton deployed. At Siccar Point there is the lonely shore, the rocks and one's thoughts. If, like Playfair, we can realise 'how much further reason may sometimes go than imagination can venture to follow', that is sufficient memorial to a great thinker.

CHAPTER 5

The Grand Staircase

AFTER THE SECOND WORLD WAR normality was not immediately restored – indeed it never was. Food continued to be rationed for several years and there were shortages of many commodities, some of them intellectual, like books. Shining like a good deed in a naughty world was the American National Geographic Magazine, with its yellow-margined cover, heavy glossy paper and colour photography. I was fortunate in that an aunt subscribed to the magazine and passed on a bundle of copies from time to time, thus helping me to form a world view at an early age.

A 1948 article about the great natural wonders of the United States knocked me sideways but, for whatever reason, going there to see for myself never occurred to me. Not until I was given the opportunity to share the suite of the organiser of a huge conference in Salt Lake City on Radiation Oncology did it become a possibility. Here was a chance to study the Mormons in their own territory and the key to exploring some of the most stunning landscapes in the world.

Utah is a big state and the first leg of the journey was in a little 36-seater plane to Saint George, 300 miles away in the extreme south-west. The culture shocks started early as we flew over vast tracts of semi-desert with no trees, no water, no people, the only slight trace of them being the Interstate Highway which the pilot was following. For me, there was the excitement of seeing, far below, the ranks of wave-cut beach terraces of the former Lake Bonneville. Lake Bonneville was 1,000 feet deep and two-thirds of the size of Scotland. As part of the Great Basin, its water did not reach the sea. The Great Salt Lake is its main vestige. Only 30 feet deep, it is bound to evaporate completely soon.

Landing was almost as terrifying as driving over military roads in the Alpes Maritimes. In this part of Utah are many buttes – flat-topped hills with near-vertical sides. Saint George airstrip was on one of these, so narrow that, sitting in a passenger seat, the town was clear hundreds of feet below on the left. As we hurtled south the runway got even narrower – but the pilot knew his job. At that time the good people of Saint George were about to get a new airport which would take bigger planes and not be closed every five minutes because of updraughts (or updrafts as they have in Utah). It was, however, going to be seven boring miles out in the desert and I feel I got the better bargain. It is an unusual experience also just to walk out of the airport, down a kind of ramp, and into the town.

Saint George has nothing to do with England or dragons. I had forgotten where I was – Utah, the land of the Latter Day Saints, where George had founded a new settlement around 1910 and named it after himself!

Unusual, also, was it to pick up my hire car, a high, wide and handsome Grand Jeep Cherokee, or whatever – the smallest available. As a safe medium saloon driver at home it was exhilarating (and dangerous!) to be a king of the road, but a little disconcerting, in Cedar City, to turn off on to a Scenic Byway to see huge signs warning me of snow and ice on an unpatrolled road in late September. ('Road not plowed in winter'.) I had forgotten that Salt Lake City had hosted the Winter Olympics and that I was headed for National Parks at 6,000 to 8,000 feet.

The first target was Bryce Canyon. Like most of the big National Parks its extent is much greater than the ordinary visitor can cover but he is cleverly manoeuvred into the best and least sensitive areas. The whole area is part of the Colorado Plateau and the accessible part of the National Park is an 18-mile road along the rim of the plateau, with frequent viewpoints and trailheads.

The views are, quite simply, stunning. Photos taken per visitor must be among the highest in the world. The reason is uniform diversity, or diverse uniformity. Geologically, Bryce Canyon is made of a particular soft sandstone from Tertiary times, which has been very evenly uplifted. As a semi-desert area with little vegetation cover, occasional torrential rain and severe frost action in winter, erosion has been rapid and uniform over large areas. But in detail, large blocks of hillside have been further cut into a myriad of 'hoodoos' (pinnacles), with the occasional natural bridge. Given the changing desert light and the yellow, white and pink cliffs the Canyon is 'like a photographer's painted studio backdrop'.

For me, with limited time, the high spots were the Bristlecone Pine Trail (1,600 years old, the oldest living things on earth), the 80-mile view over the Grand Staircase and the sunset from Sunset Point. Next morning it was Fairyland Point and the Fairyland Loop Trail – rather twee names for grandeur which might become terrifying in bad weather. (When the original Ebenezer Bryce was being quizzed about the canyon his comment was – 'It's a hell of a place to lose a cow'.) Hot and dusty, with no water but a sensational view around every corner, I met two people in a morning – and this in a Park with 1.5 million visitors annually.

Bryce Canyon is a wonderful place, with a host of fascinating details which require no special knowledge to appreciate. For me an added wonder is its size and its uniformity. Coming from Scotland where practically every inch of the country has been squeezed and twisted, broken, sunk beneath the sea and raised again, it is difficult to contemplate the vast simplicity of Bryce and the Colorado Plateau. We have to take on board a huge lake the size of four states, filled with uniform sediments which were then lifted almost perfectly horizontally to their present condition.

Off now to Zion National Park, which is in two parts and where, again, the general public are admitted to only a small part of the whole. The total area of the park is 229 square miles, but almost everyone is limited to the Zion Canyon Scenic Drive. At Bryce most visitors are on the high plateau looking around and down; most visitors to Zion are in the valley of the North Fork of the Virgin River looking up two to three thousand feet to the most impressive mountains. The first Mormon pioneers in the 1860s acknowledged that they were in the presence of the Sublime as they named this new land. Zion itself, Temple of the Sun, The Great White Throne, Angels Landing, Cathedral Mountain, the Three Patriarchs (Abraham, Isaac and Joseph), Towers of the Virgin, Kolob (a Mormon holy place near to God) – reflect the awe and wonder felt by these early settlers and everyone since. (I have no hypothesis about the naming of Refrigerator Canyon, unless it is a symptom of the growth of consumerism in the 20th century).

Access is much more strictly controlled than at Bryce. At the park entrance is a Visitor Center and here one leaves one's car. A shuttle bus runs the six miles up the Zion Canyon Scenic Drive to Temple of Sinawava. There are five shuttle stops at which one can get out to admire the view, or 'take a picture' as the Americans say, or walk around for a bit, or walk to another stop, or back to the centre.

Coming from the east along the Zion–Mount Carmel Highway, the road is at almost 6,000 feet in slickrock country, with masses of bare white, orange and red sandstone eroded into fantastic shapes. Checkerboard Mesa has an amazingly regular pattern of cracks and grooves which subtly changes as the sun declines. Just before the tunnel there is a Canyon Overlook Trail which takes one above the Great Arch for a first glimpse of Zion proper. Standing at mountain top level, just above the Great Arch of Zion, the huge cliffs and strange shapes are far below. Two tunnels, one over a mile long, and a series of zig-zags lead down to the visitor centre. Completed in 1930, the road was an engineering marvel in its time and was considered, according to the guidebook, 'an almost impossible project.'

My day started early with the shuttle ride to Temple of Sinawava, so early that only the mountain tops were in sunshine. A riverside walk goes upstream to Zion Canyon Narrows. In this land of violent contrasts and violent storms one must check the danger level of the Narrows before starting. Down here is one of the few damp and shady environments in this semi-desert, with hanging gardens of wildflowers.

Two shuttle bus stops downstream is the trail to Weeping Rock, another damp and shady place where the cliff overhangs a large cave, so that one can stand and gaze across at Angels Landing and The Organ through a gentle curtain of water. Trails heading up and away were tempting but too time-consuming. Even here, with 2.5 million visitors annually, there were times and places when one was on one's own.

Instead, it was down to the next stop, The Grotto, across the river and along the Kayenta Trail to the Emerald Pools. Through a kind of wonderland of blocks and passages is the Upper Emerald Pool, nestling at the foot of a monstrous cliff and ending by a smooth, polished rock surface which curves over the edge of more cliffs below. Imagine my anxiety, a few minutes later, when I met a blind man with a dog and a little girl marching resolutely towards this hazard. From the west side of the valley there are stupendous views across to the Great White Throne and Mountain of the Sun. The next stop of the shuttle gives access to a viewpoint looking west, to The Beehives, The Sentinel, The Court of the Patriarchs and the Three Patriarchs themselves.

Salt Lake City called, but on the way back to St George I was able to fit in the Johnson Farm Dinosaur Track Site. In the Jurassic period the land in this location was at or near sea level and thick mud along the shore began to dry. Animals came in to eat and drink. Their footprints were preserved. Mud cracks developed and, as the lake level rose, a thick bed of sand covered the surface. Ripple marks reflected the waves on the shore and the sand hardened into sandstone. The result was an astonishing assemblage of fossil remains and tracks.

Within the Johnson Farm boundary there are at least four distinct layers containing dinosaur tracks and there are three more dinosaur track horizons just outside. Fossil fish, shellfish and plants abound. Identifying dinosaur footprints is difficult, but three definite species have been identified, one about 20 feet long. Five other types of footprint await classification. *Batrachopus,* whose tracks have been found here, was not a dinosaur but a small upright-walking reptile like a crocodile.

The sheer quantity of remains is staggering. Laid out in the desert sun are rows of stone blocks with ripple marks, mud cracks and salt casts. Footprints of all shapes and sizes abound, with some quite special items. On one rock are detailed impressions of a dinosaur's skin. In a dinosaur trackway is the very rare trace where the tail has dragged on the surface. A dinosaur swimming in shallow water might leave traces on the lake bed – such swim tracks can be seen on several rocks. Proudly the Leisure Services Department of St George states that:

> The only other known specimen of a swim track is from rocks of about the same age in the Connecticut Valley.

Johnson Farm is a quite astonishing place. There can be nothing to beat it for quality as well as for quantity. The evidence is fresh and sharp and even the most obtuse of observers must be drawn in to speculation about these creatures and what they were up to. There is, also, the irony that we can learn more here about life on Earth 200 million years ago than we can learn about our ancestors in historical times.

The question is: where was the Grand Staircase in all this? And the answer is – all around. I just didn't have the perspective to see it. Like a mite in a stair carpet, I was too small and too close to see the big, big picture. If we go back to Sunset Point above Bryce Canyon, at 8,000 feet looking east we see long stretches of horizontal plateau 50 to 80 miles away, amazingly regular but with an occasional step down to the next flat stretch to the south. From Rainbow Point (9,115 feet) on the Bristlecone Loop Trail, looking west, we see the changes in slope even better. The Paunsaugunt Plateau surface is forested. Then we see the bare rock Pink Cliffs which continue the spectacular forms of Bryce. And then we are down to the next – forested – level.

The Colorado Plateau is a vast simplicity, with layer upon layer of sediments laid down consistently and uplifted without any substantial faulting or deformation. The youngest rocks are Tertiary at about 8,000 feet at Bryce Canyon. The bottom layer at Bryce is the top layer at Zion, at about 6,000 feet. There are eight main layers of rock in Zion, their varying textures and colours reflecting changes in conditions as they were being deposited. Of them the 2,000-foot cliffs of the Navajo Sandstone are believed to be the tallest sandstone cliffs in the world.

The bottom layer at Zion becomes the top layer at the North Rim of the Grand Canyon, 120 miles to the south. How simple it all is! Tertiary at the top, Cretaceous in the middle, Jurassic at the bottom – just like a diagram in a book. And great masses of uniform rock. And such rock, clean and colourful, some so rough that one can walk up steep slopes, hands in one's pockets. And so easy to study – little vegetation and no real farming. So unlike our poor old Scotland, with practically every corner fractured and twisted.

How young it all is! In Scotland only a few scraps of landscape survive from the Jurassic and Cretaceous, in Skye and in little patches on either side of the Moray Firth. Lowland Britain is where we must seek the Jurassic dinosaurs – in Dorset and north Yorkshire – and the accumulated remains of countless sea creatures – as at Beachy Head.

But this very simplicity increases the wonder with which one contemplates the Grand Staircase. This enormous landmass, formed beneath seas and lakes, has floated upwards for over a mile without tilting or deformation, with no significant faulting or volcanic activity. 'The mind grows giddy.' One can imagine Caspar David Friedrich's Silent Watcher on a viewpoint in Bryce Canyon. Chet Raymo, author of *The Crust of Our Earth: An Armchair Traveler's Guide to the New Geology,* 't'best book on t'soobject', probably unconsciously uses Playfair's words when describing the revelations of Hutton at Siccar Point – 'The Abyss of Time' – as his heading for the section on the Grand Canyon.

Back in Salt Lake City it might have been possible to look with satisfaction at this escapade. Another target achieved. Some marvellous experiences. One or two very mild adventures. One moment – but only one – of sheer panic. Some unanticipated discoveries.

Yet there remains a touch of unease. This trip was run against the clock and a loose end remains. Angels Landing (5,990 feet) is a spectacular peak from which the views would be astounding. Access is not easy, shuttle bus to The Grotto, cross the river and follow the West Rim Trail through Refrigerator Canyon. Then climb Walter's Wiggles – who could resist those? – to Scout Lookout and Angels Landing Trail to the top. As the Park Guide says:

> **Strenuous.** Long dropoffs and narrow trails. Not for anyone fearful of heights. Ends at summit high above Zion Canyon floor. Last 0.5 mile follows a steep narrow ridge; chains have been added for safety.

Who could resist the challenge?

Earlier we stood behind Caspar David Friedrich's Silent Watcher as he contemplated the chalk cliffs of Rügen, marvelling at the work of God, or later in life, reflecting on the dynamic processes that had turned myriads of tiny creatures into solid rock. The huge area I have called the Grand Staircase is so vast and so uniform it is almost impossible for us to come to terms with it.

No doubt the Native Americans had their creation myths to explain all they found there. In Albert Bierstadt (1830–1902) the United States had its own Friedrich, who went west to find vast landscapes towering over a few tiny men, especially in the Sierra Nevada of California. As we have seen, the Mormons who colonised south Utah were so over-whelmed by the majesty of the valley of the North Fork of the Virgin River, and the mountains around, that they called it Zion – the hill on which the city of Jerusalem stood and, by extension, Heaven, the city of God and 'the final abode of the elect'.

Angels Landing is one of the Mormons' special places and the approach to it threw me back to the 17th century and John Bunyan's *Pilgrim's Progress*. Mr Christian goes through many trials, tribulations and temptations before making it to the Celestial City and eventual salvation. In the Slough of Despond he is completely bogged down by the weight of his sins – and the way to Angels Landing starts by crossing the river and marshes. Christian is beset by many temptations on the way – and Refrigerator Canyon can be symbolic of the dangers of consumerism and of gulping unwisely when overcome by heat. Walter's Wiggles are a series of traverses making it possible to climb the side of a ridge slowly, but without excessive effort.

'Strait is the way...' but the true pilgrim sees the Holy City and marches resolutely towards it. Deviation is a sign of weakness, a lack of faith. To follow 'Walter's Wiggles' is to admit to the butterfly mind, to being easily distracted, to a weakness of character, to the possibility of turning back. Nevertheless, Scout Lookout is eventually attained and the way to the Celestial City seems clear, if vertiginous. However, all day it has been oppressively hot and the late afternoon is the time for hot gusts of wind to sweep the pilgrim off the steep narrow ridge. 'Chains have been added for safety' – but the regular lightning strikes at about 4pm make them a distinct hazard!

At Angels Landing the pilgrim receives his spiritual reward – a towering feeling of being right next to Heaven and surrounded by glorious peaks and cliffs and canyons.

CHAPTER 6

On Hearing the First Delius of Spring

THE THOUGHTS MAY seem random, but the execution of the quest is usually carefully planned. Every now and again, however, the quest itself just happens and would be of no particular interest to an outsider. What one recalls is an encounter with a stranger or some other diversion along the way.

For this quest the date is important. It is 22 May and the objective is Beinn a'Chaisgein Mor in Wester Ross. Base camp is the Loch Maree Hotel, that splendid survivor of another era. On the south shore of Loch Maree – not as obvious as it seems, since the settlement at the head of Loch Maree is called Kinlochewe[1] – the hotel seems little changed from 1877 when Queen Victoria stayed there or when the guests picked up their poisoned sandwiches in the 1920s.

The day's objective is in the wild tangle of lochs and mountains between Loch Maree and Little Loch Broom. Sometimes called 'The Last Wilderness', more prosaically it includes the Dundonnell, Letterewe and Fisherfield deer forests and the area where Frank Fraser Darling spent two years among the red deer. The first person to study large mammals in their own territory, his *A Herd of Red Deer* was the first book of its kind. It superbly combines accurate observation with a sensitive awareness of the landscape and the beauty of our largest native animal.

This last great wilderness in Britain is an area of high rugged mountains, of bare rock pavements and stony glens, of moors and bogs, of waterfalls, difficult river crossings and a multitude of lochs of every shape and size. There are no roads here, nor are there any longer any permanent human dwellings. All but one of the mountains had been climbed and today was the day to finish off with The Hill of the Big Cheese (Beinn a'Chaisgein Mor) – or is it The Big Hill of Cheese?

The way in began with a run of about fifteen miles in the car, followed by a couple of miles on the bike until a substantial fence indicated that the landowner (now deceased) was very happy for his estate to be open to walkers, but to walkers only – despite the definition by the Court of Session of the bicycle as 'an aid to pedestrianism'. The next two miles were easy and pleasant enough, to be followed by about three miles of trackless, miserable morass, followed in turn by one of those magical places one finds in the Highlands. A basin of beautiful lochs was surrounded by great peaks and fearsome cliffs, all linked by a network of splendid stalkers' tracks.

Over to the right, just about where the valley side was roughening up to become the 2000-foot cliffs of Ben Lair ('the finest, and probably the longest, mountain wall in the Highlands'), was a little patch of scrub woodland – little more than a few gorse bushes – yet what should be emerging into the clear air but the familiar, irritating, call of the cuckoo.

The cuckoo is a distinctive bird in several ways, not perhaps, in appearance – which is unknown to most – but certainly in its call. I claim no great expertise in the determination of bird song but, to quote from a hillwalker's guide to the landscape and wildlife of Scotland's mountain environment:

> Cuckoos are probably the only British bird that most people could identify by call alone, and this is certainly the easiest way to detect them. (*Hostile Habitats: Scotland's Mountain Environment,* eds. Kempe and Wrightman, Scottish Mountaineering Trust, 2006)

The cuckoo is one of the few species which is usually identified by its call which, as everyone knows, is the repetition of its name – or rather its name is the repetition of its call. Hence its scientific name Cuculus, whose appropriateness is rivalled only by that of the corncrake (Crex crex). In Germany it is the Kuckuck: in the Netherlands the Koekoek. In France it is the Coucou and in Sweden the Gök. In Gaelic it is the Cuthag.

Added to the distinctiveness of its call we have also its dysfunctional family life, with the oversized young being fed by overworked foster parents. It performs huge migrations, spending its winters in Africa and its summers in northern Europe. Once it has fledged, the young cuckoo is on its own and must make its way to and from Africa without any assistance; in fact, it never knowingly sees its real parents, who have usually departed for Africa before the fledgling chick has left the nest.

The result is a bird of character, around which has been woven much creative thinking, usually based on its cheerful announcement of spring. The cuckoo clock stridently measures the passage of time. One of the many tales of folly fathered on the Wise Men of Gotham was that they joined hands round a thorn bush to shut in a cuckoo, thereby ensuring a permanent summer. In Gotham is a pub sign to prove it!

For more than seven centuries the Anglo-Saxons have sung:

Sumer is icumen in,
Lhude sing cuccu!
Sing cuccu, nu, sing cuccu,
Sing cuccu, sing cuccu, nu!

In a sonnet Edmund Spenser (1552–1599) wrote of: 'The merry cuckoo, messenger of Spring.'

Wordsworth in *To the Cuckoo* referred to the difficulty of seeing it:

O Cuckoo! Shall I call thee bird,
Or but a wandering voice?

And in *The Solitary Reaper* showed that he knew of its widespread distribution:

A voice so thrilling ne'er was heard,
In spring-time from the Cuckoo-bird,
Breaking the silence of the seas
Among the furthest Hebrides.

Shakespeare also referred to its invisibility:

He was but as the cuckoo is in June,
Heard, not regarded.

And to its doubtful morality:

The cuckoo then, on every tree,
Mocks married men: for thus sings he,
Cuckoo;
Cuckoo, cuckoo; O word of fear
Unpleasing to a married ear!

Musicians have brought in the cuckoo when they wished to celebrate spring and the outdoors. When Respighi fashioned from 18th century harpsichord pieces his suite *The Birds*, those he chose to illustrate or imitate were the hen, the dove, the nightingale and – the cuckoo, which gently persists against a background of twittering woodland birds. An orchestral colleague recently played and sang a mediaeval Italian song about spring and the cuckoo; she declined to translate on the grounds that the company was mixed!

Beethoven's *Sixth Symphony* – the 'Pastoral' – is the only one in which he gives the movements names. In the slow movement (*By the Brook*), after a long and sublimely beautiful ripple he brings in some bird calls, including a tree-softened cuckoo. While Vaughan Williams gave us *The Lark Ascending* to epitomise the English countryside, Delius in *On Hearing the First Cuckoo of Spring* wrote a warm, gentle evocation of green woods and misty meadows, with the cuckoo barely heard but quietly insistent in the distance. In Humperdinck's *Hänsel und Gretel* it is the cuckoo – the egg-thief and murderer – who warns the children of the evils of theft as they pick forbidden strawberries in the forest.

WH Davies called the cuckoo 'the simple bird that thinks two notes a song' and at one time there was quite a vogue for 'Toy Symphonies' using a small two-note wind instrument called a cuckoo. Traditionally Haydn is supposed to have bought some toy instruments at a fair and written a score for them for the court at Esterházy. Mozart's father's *Toy Symphony* will be familiar to those who watch show-jumping on television. The *Oxford Companion to Music* lists another 13 composers who composed 'Toy Symphonies', including Mendelssohn, who wrote two, now lost – perhaps just as well.

Opus 336 of Johann Strauss II (1825–1899) was a high-speed, energetic polka, a tribute to the countryside the Viennese knew best. It was first performed in St Petersburg as *In the Pavlovsk Woods*. Back in Vienna it was *Im Krapfenwandl*, Josef Krapf being the keeper of a popular tavern in the Vienna woods. In the English-speaking world it became the jolly *Cuckoo Polka* in which the virtuoso musician (on the cuckoo) makes no fewer than eight entries in each of the four main sections and five more in the coda – to be rewarded with tumultuous applause at the close.

In the days of the popular song – as opposed to the pop song – there was the *Cuckoo Waltz*, with the immortal words: 'Cuckoo, cuckoo. I think I am going daft!' There was also: 'Sing a song, sing a song, Mr Cuckoo.' The catchy rhythm of the *Cuckoo Song* is recognised by millions who have no idea of its title, nor that it was specially written for a Laurel and Hardy film.

To quote, prosaically, from *Hostile Habitats* again:

Common enough on the lower slopes of many Scottish hills, cuckoos are a welcome addition to the summer scene, although sometimes, perhaps, a little too obvious. They have been recorded calling up to 300 times in succession, but any camper woken on a May morning by a particularly persistent cuckoo must feel this record could easily be broken by anyone who could be bothered to keep counting.

We know the Victorian child was meant to be seen and not heard. By contrast, the cuckoo is frequently heard, but very seldom seen. My own sightings have been well spaced out, the first I remember being over 50 years ago near the T Wood, just south of Edinburgh. There, on a Sunday morning, our family watched the flutterings of the biggish grey bird as it worked the fringes of the wood in search of a suitable – mate or host? Now the spread of suburban housing and the longest artificial ski slope in Europe militate against a large population of the little birds the cuckoo was wont to bully into acting as foster parents for her brood. In recent years I have probably been in Wester Ross a dozen times since I was last by the T Wood. For me, the call of the cuckoo has become synonymous with Highland glens in the late spring – and with being unable to sleep after 4am because of the wretched bird.

Another sighting of the cuckoo, about ten years ago, was almost as far as one could get from Edinburgh and still be on the Scottish mainland, at Durness in north-west Sutherland. Here is a gaunt, bare, limestone landscape with great sea-cliffs – and only one tree. Just outside the village, to the east, it is about 25 feet high and is surrounded by drystane dykes and decayed croftland. In flight the cuckoo looks rather hawk-like with long pointed wings and long tail, like a rather soft sparrow hawk. However, its flight is weak and it is a cause for amazement that such a poor flyer should be able to make two huge journeys every year, from and to its African wintering grounds.

'Wing and prayer fail to save young osprey' was an October headline when one of three Loch Garten osprey chicks 'ran out of fuel and simply couldn't keep flying' after 2,000 miles. When this can happen to such a big, powerful bird how can we fail to admire the cuckoo, modestly plodding its 6,000-mile round trip for generation after generation?

And there was the Durness Cuckoo, making sad little forays from the tree, 20 yards on to a dyke, or 30 yards to a patch of sedge, but returning always to the imagined security of the tree. For half an hour it could clearly be seen, obviously unhappy but unable to make anything of the unprepossessing environment.

Between the writing of the preceding pages and their revision I witnessed the most remarkable sight. In the Central Highlands there is a huge quadrangle, whose corners are at Spean Bridge, Dalwhinnie, Blair Atholl and Crianlarich. Within the quadrangle are dozens of the highest mountains in Britain, scores of lochs and great expanses of moorland – but scarcely a house and hardly a road. It is the homeland of the red deer and the golden eagle yet the West Highland railway line provides access for walkers and climbers, only 12 hours from Euston by overnight sleeper.

On 27 May 2010, I was trudging back to Corrour station and passed the head of Loch Treig, where there is a shooting lodge and a vestigial block of Scots Pines. At about four o'clock the afternoon chorus of cuckoos started up. No surprise in this. Normal for the time of day and season. Then I heard a particularly insistent cuckoo call coming from over my left shoulder and swung round to see, not one, but two cuckoos, about 20 yards off. The female was flying hell for leather southward, pursued by the male, who was calling all the time. About 200 yards ahead she doubled back, only for him to follow suit and the loving couple disappeared back towards Loch Treig.

Given the rarity with which even a single cuckoo is spotted, and the even greater rarity with which the laying of a cuckoo's egg has been captured on film, I feel I have been tremendously privileged to have witnessed what might very loosely be described as the courtship of these unconventional birds. Not perhaps a Random Thought, but it obviously pays to be a Random Fellow.

But to return to 22 May in Wester Ross. About five o'clock, tired but complacent at having, once more, successfully avoided trouble, I passed again my little scrap of shrubland beside the Fionn Loch to hear the repetitive cuckoo for the nth time. That set me thinking – how could such a feeble bird get to such an isolated place? Then came my first startling revelation; from the Loch Maree Hotel to the Fionn Loch might be a giant step for this specimen of mankind, but for the cuckoo it was a mere four miles by air. What was wildness to me was to him a perfectly acceptable summer habitat.

I wondered at the bird's thought processes. Imagine having flown from Africa, perhaps to the south-west of England; then pressing north, perhaps through the great forests of the Welsh borderland and lush Shropshire, on through Lancashire and Cumbria to the forests of the Borders and the southern Highlands. Onward, ever onward – and the journey comes to this, a single tree on the edge of the northern sea or a scrap of shrub in a mountain wilderness. Does a great flock of cuckoos fly north, dropping off one by one as each in succession finds a cuckoo-free habitat? So that the one who eventually makes it to Durness is probably the slowest, or the least aggressive?

One can understand a migratory urge, forcing a bird northward, ever northward but, as well as being found all over Europe in summer (even in Orkney and Shetland, although not in the Faeroes and Iceland). the cuckoo is widespread over Ireland, leading to further speculation. How do the cuckoos get there? From Brittany, over 300 miles of sea to the south coast? Or do they press on north over England and turn off at right angles to head for the short-sea crossings from Great Britain – Fishguard to Rosslare? Holyhead to Dun Laoghaire? Stranraer to Larne? Or the older and shorter Portpatrick to Donaghadee ferry crossing? And how do they know when to turn left?

We can all remember, when there used to be telephone wires in the countryside, flocks of swallows congregating and twittering until, one day, all of a sudden, they were gone, off to Africa for the winter. In the flock there would be first-timers and experienced travellers, the latter operating from memory and from whom the young ones could learn to add memory to instinct. For the swallow, migration is a social experience, but the young cuckoo does not know its biological parents and cannot learn by imitating them. How can a solitary youngster navigate its way to Africa? Or, rather, to a precise spot in that vast continent? And back again, to one tree in the extreme north-west of Europe?

It is perhaps easiest to understand when we recall that, isolate though the cuckoo may be, it is extremely sensitive to the behaviour of other birds. Like us, it must be acutely aware of shortening days and cooler temperatures in late summer. Any bird capable of choosing the nest of one species to parasitise, of laying an egg which matches the eggs of the targeted host and ejecting the one egg necessary to make space for its own, is bound to be conscious of the late summer behaviour of other birds like the swallow – the gathering together as the days become shorter, the heightened tension and the southward departure. The cuckoo must feel a pressure to behave similarly. It may not join a flock but it does join the great mass movement southwards at the end of summer.

Research on the cuckoo has a long history. When Darwin was at Edinburgh University he was elected to the Plinian Society, at which, in 1826, two separate papers on the cuckoo were read. Much of the recent research on the cuckoo has involved reed warblers in the Fens near Cambridge. The reed warbler is a summer visitor and it is very likely that, in the autumn, the young cuckoo's attachment to its foster parents results in its tagging along behind when the great migration begins. The reed warbler is not found in Wester Ross, but the sedge warbler is, and is likely to be the preferred choice for the Wester Ross cuckoo. Its habitat is in bushy places and in coarse vegetation fairly near water, making it an accessible victim on which the cuckoo can impose its offspring. Again, one can see the young cuckoo tagging along when the time comes to fly off south.

According to JTR Sharrock in *The Atlas of Breeding Birds in Britain and Ireland* (British Trust for Ornithology and Irish Wildbird Conservancy, Tring, 1976):

> The female returns to the same area in consecutive years and concentrates on a particular host species, normally the one which was her own foster parent.

That is clear enough and we can work out how it happens – observation of the gathering grounds as the year progresses in Africa, a timetable parallel to that of the other migrants and an instinctive drive to the north. On this journey, however, instinct is supported by an element of observation and memory of the autumn journey south.

Now, however, another tricky question comes up. During the Ice Age most of Britain north of the Thames was covered by ice. It could be that the cuckoo was to be found in summer in the extreme south of England but not till the ice vanished could there be adequate vegetation and associated food elsewhere for a bird like the cuckoo. Wester Ross had its own Readvance before the ice finally (we think!) disappeared about 11,500 years ago and the area was recolonised by vegetation and animal life. So think of today's cuckoo. If it is a female she has returned to the place she originated from. But her female parent must have originated in the same place, and hers, and hers. So, to put it in human family terms, today's female Fionn Loch Cuckoo is directly descended in the female line from the first female cuckoo to parasitise an innocent wee bird shortly after the post-glacial greening of that environment. A staggering thought – how many generations have filled the air in this spot with the same old two notes? Standing by the lochside, the mind grows giddy thinking of the persistence of this seemingly puny bird over thousands of years. What is oneself compared with this wonderful durability and will to live?

Yet it cannot be as simple as the experts suggest. If the female simply returned to the area of her birth there could be no expansion of the range of the species: when the ice vanished there would have been a vacuum of female cuckoos between Sussex and Wester Ross. If we look again, more closely, at the distribution map for the cuckoo we note, however, that, while the cuckoo breeds in Orkney and Shetland, only occasional visitors reach the Faeroes and Iceland. This seems to suggest that males range further than females in their search for mates and are probably blown off course from time to time. Some day a Shetland-bound female will be blown to the Faeroes, meet a male and the following year the progeny will return to set up a new migration pattern.

It seems likely that this process of accidental colonisation would account for the gradual spread of the cuckoo from southern England till all the British Isles felt the presence of the 'wandering voice'. By a lonely lochside in Wester Ross one can only marvel at the ingenuity and persistence of this remarkable bird and, like it, rejoice in the coming of spring and the conclusion of its formidable journey.

Note

1 Kinlochewe means 'At the head of Loch Ewe', but is at the head of the freshwater Loch Maree. Poolewe is where the River Ewe falls into the sea, here called Loch Ewe.

CHAPTER 7

Lines on a Map

WHEN I STARTED TEACHING Geography I was very lucky in that there was a revolution going on in teaching methods and in textbooks. Maps, photos, diagrams and sketches were in; blocks of descriptive text were out. The sample study was in; woolly generalisation on a continental scale was out.

As the name implies, a sample study was a case study typical of an area, which could be closely examined and from which wider generalisations could be made. A particular favourite of mine was a farm near Sevenoaks in Kent. The farm was where the Upper Greensand and Gault clay – complete with brickworks – met the chalk of the North Downs. The farmer had orchards and grew soft fruit and cereals. (He may even had had a dairying operation.) From the map one could deduce why each field was used the way it was – nature of the soil, slope of the land, proximity to farm buildings and market(s), and so on. It was all beautifully satisfying – intellectually.

One July I was due to attend a markers' meeting in London on a Monday and set off a couple of days early so that I could take in some walking on the North Downs and Lullingstone Roman villa. I would start at Sevenoaks and get some slides of the sample farm, which would help to enliven my teaching next winter.

Imagine my horror when I got there to find that the orchards had been cleared, the hedges grubbed up and the entire acreage was an expanse of barley, waving in the wind. What about the sensitive adjustment of the cropping pattern to geology and relief? The fine-grained farmscape had been replaced by a monoculture based on the use of heavy machinery. For a couple of years I had been teaching a lie, teaching something that may have been environmental history but was certainly not the truth about today's world.

Nor was I alone. All over Britain and in other English-speaking countries – the series was especially popular in India – teachers were doggedly getting their pupils to make connections which were no longer relevant. This was worrying – and how many other examples of the same kind of problem were we blithely passing on to those in our charge?

I was especially worried about my slide of La Jonction, which I had taken about ten years previously and found very useful in helping people to visualise a phenomenon invisible to the naked eye. The problem simmered for years till it became insupportable and I decided I had to go back and check that all was as it ought to be. This was no random quest but a purposeful search.

In the west end of the city of Geneva, which is really its East End, is a feature known as La Jonction (see PLATE 3A). Not many tourists make it to this spot, situated as it is at the end of an unsalubrious area with the former gasworks, a sewage treatment plant and the former tram depot with the tram drivers' houses. But anyone who does make it to the point, or to the railway bridge from which the photo was taken, sees a quite remarkable sight.

The River Rhône rises in the upper Valais of Switzerland and flows into the Lake of Geneva, where the sediment it has carried down from the mountains is deposited. Geneva is situated at the west end of the lake and the overflow becomes the lower Rhône, eventually running into the Mediterranean.

From the slopes of Mont Blanc and the Chamonix area comes the Arve, full of grit and fine sediment from the Alpine glaciers, to join the Rhône at La Jonction. The contrast between the clear water of the Rhône on the left (north) and the milky waters of the Arve is startling. What is almost as remarkable is the sharp line dividing them and the fact (which the reader must take on trust) that this sharp line continues for about a kilometre downstream. (When I saw this first in 1958 the junction was unencumbered but unfortunately a sewer has been constructed since then. It looks like a wall separating the two streams but its top is just below the water level and a little of the Rhône water can be seen creeping over to join the Arve.) The streams do not easily mix because of their differing densities – the result of the Arve sediment – and temperatures – the Arve comes straight out of the glaciers while the Rhône water has had a long journey on which it has been warming up.

For many years I used a slide of La Jonction as a kind of visual metaphor for the line on a weather map we call a Front. We think of the atmosphere as being invisible and loose and uncontrolled – 'free as air', we say, 'free as the wind'. 'The wind bloweth as it listeth', said St John. Yet, at the same time, we have been conscious of differences between different kinds of air – 'the north wind doth blow and we shall have snow', says the old rhyme. However, the systematic and measurable differentiation between masses of atmosphere was a 20th century concept developed by Bjerknes and the 'Bergen School' of meteorology from 1917.

Élisée Reclus was a geographer and one of the 'Outlook Tower' circle of Patrick Geddes. Exiled from France for his part in the Commune he wandered around western Europe teaching and activating. The beginning of scientific weather forecasting lay in the realisation by Reclus that there was a semi-permanent Azores anticyclone and that this had an important influence on the weather of western Europe. If one knew what the weather was like in the Azores today, one could forecast with some accuracy when that weather would reach us and what it would be like. Reclus won the support of Albert 1 of Monaco and in 1893 an underwater cable was laid to transmit information from five stations in the Azores to the Paris observatory.[1]

The contribution of the Bergen School was to define large areas of the world where the air acquired common characteristics of tempera-ture, humidity and pressure. From a source area such as the mid-Atlantic a great mass of air – quite cleverly called an 'air mass' – would move, displacing the air already over Britain and replacing it with the charac-teristics of Maritime Tropical air. It seems unlikely, but an air mass can retain its integrity over hundreds of miles and for several weeks – a little like the rivers in Geneva.

Equally surprising is that these air masses, when they come against each other, do not immediately mix. Just as the Arve and the Rhône have a clear line separating them, adjacent air masses can be clearly differentiated. The line separating two air masses is called a front and can be drawn on a map, but is seldom seen in the sky. Yet we can all sense a change in the weather. In Edinburgh it suddenly becomes warm and muggy and one can smell the distilleries. Or one can stand on the top of Arthur's Seat and look to the north-west, to see the brilliant clarity of the light and the onset of wintry showers.

Fronts, of course, exist in three dimensions and the line on the map shows where the two air masses meet on the earth's surface. One air mass may be sliding over another, or be being undercut by another, resulting in a front sloping up to 50km. This means that we can look up and estimate the approach of a front by the appearance of the clouds – first high-level, then medium-level, then low cloud, by which time it is probably raining and the wind has changed direction.

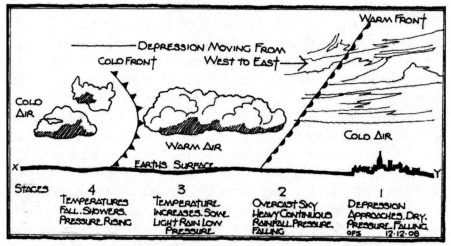

FIG. 6 A Mid-latitude Depression.

Warm fronts mean warmer air, usually moist, and steady rain. Cold fronts bring colder air and showers, often heavy, with brilliant intervals. Occluded fronts (not shown above) mean trouble. Rain is continuous and heavy. An occlusion often stagnates, hanging around for several days.

An isotherm is a line drawn on a map joining places with the same temperature. Two isotherms combine to give us a rough and ready understanding of temperatures anywhere in the British Isles.

The July isotherm for 15°C runs across Ireland from Galway Bay to Strangford Lough, south of Belfast, across the Isle of Man, through the Lake District to just north of the mouth of the Tees. This means that, on an average taken over many years, everywhere south of this line has a July temperature of over 15°C, while, north of the line, July is cooler than 15°C. This fact will surprise nobody, as we all know that, in our latitude, the further south we go, the higher the sun is in the sky and the more powerful it is. In the days when county cricketers all played for the county they were born in, Neville Cardus commented that the men of Sussex were always browner than the rest.

The winter picture is quite different. The January isotherm for 4°C runs almost due south from Durness, keeping a few miles inland from the west coast till it cuts off Galloway, skirts the Lake District and the Lancashire coast, heads south along the English-Welsh border, loops up the Severn almost to Birmingham, then round almost to the English Channel in Hampshire. It runs eastward a few miles north of the English Channel till it runs out of land at the North Foreland in Kent. (In order that temperatures in different places can be compared with each other they are reduced to sea level. In other words, Britain is treated as if it were a flat plain – which it is not! If we think of Fort William and the summit of Ben Nevis, the average temperature difference is 12°C.)

There is clearly a division between west and east. The *Arbutus* (strawberry tree) is a native of the Mediterranean. In Portugal its fruits give a potent spirit. It has an out-station in Brittany. In Ireland it is confined to the south-west but featured in a Victorian ballad – *My Love's an Arbutus*. Inverewe is an exotic oasis in the gaunt rocky landscape of Wester Ross and all down the west coast, through Argyll to Galloway, to north Wales and Cornwall, there are great gardens with plants totally out of place in such northern latitudes, latitudes the same as frozen Labrador. Where did our early potatoes come from before globalisation? Ayrshire, Pembroke and Cornwall.

By contrast, how often does snow in Kent hit the headlines? When cold winds from the east hit high ground in Aberdeenshire, Northumberland, the North York Moors, the Lincolnshire Wolds the snow-ploughs are out and the overhead cables are down. East Anglia can be frost-bound for long periods.

In winter this east-west contrast is explained by the differing temperatures of the seas around Britain and of the air masses which have been warmed – or cooled – by passing over them. The Gulf Stream and North Atlantic Drift are great moving carpets of warm water originating in the Gulf of Mexico, sweeping past our western shores and warming our south-westerly winds from below. Where there is a gap in the western barrier of hills, as between the Welsh mountains and the Cotswolds, the warm air can penetrate a long way inland. On the other hand, as any North Berwick bather will tell you, the North Sea is appreciably cooler than the other waters around our shores. Far from the ameliorating influence of the Atlantic the mercury in the thermometers of Eastern Europe plummets in winter so that any Polar Continental air mass (to use the jargon) from the east will be bitingly cold and dry. Passage over the North Sea will increase its instability, as will having to rise over the modest hills of eastern Britain. Hence the snow.

Putting the two isotherms together divides the British Isles into four quadrants and knowing where any place relates to these gives a pretty good idea of its temperature regime. The situation looks something like this:

Winter – mild	Winter – cold
Summer – cool	Summer – cool
Most equable	Coolest
Winter – mild	Winter – cold
Summer – hot	Summer – hot
Warmest	Most extreme

I call this the Magic Quadrant. Name me a place and I can tell you what it is like, summer and winter.

Above it was implied that there is a great deal of high ground near the west coast. Having looked at some climatic lines on the map it is now appropriate to look at the structure of our islands and see whether there are correspondingly important structural lines.

Many years ago the distinguished Welsh archaeologist Sir Cyril Fox drew a line on a map from the mouth of the Tees to the

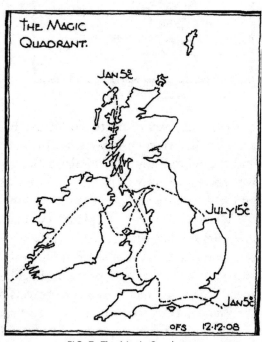

FIG. 7 The Magic Quadrant.

mouth of the Exe, dividing our islands into Highland Britain and Lowland Britain:

To the north and west of this line is the region of mountains and old rocks; to its south and east the newer fertile land of the plains. These

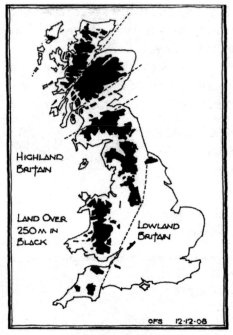

HIGHLAND
BRITAIN

LAND OVER
250 M IN
BLACK

LOWLAND
BRITAIN

OFS 12·12·08

FIG. 8 Highland Britain and Lowland Britain.

regions differ vastly in their climate, rocks, soils, scenery, plants, animals – and men.

Highland Britain has old, hard rocks, a complex geology, poor soils and, particularly in the west, a high rainfall. Lowland Britain has younger, soft rocks and a simpler geology, resulting in large stretches of similar landscape. The 'piece of chalk' we started with was a component of the chalk hills – The Chilterns, the Downs and so on – running across south-east England. To the north is the parallel Jurassic limestone belt, running from the fossil coast of Dorset, through the Cotswolds to the fossil coast of north Yorkshire. Between these great escarpments are extensive clay vales. Soils in Lowland Britain are generally base-rich and the rainfall low. In Highland Britain were many areas where coal was accessible, providing the fuel that drove the Industrial Revolution and spurred city and population growth.

When we consider wild plants, Denmark, Belgium and Lowland Britain are quite similar, with 1,030, 1,140 and 1,172 species respectively. Since our wild plants recolonised Britain from the south after the ice receded and vanished, the best parts of Highland Britain have under 1,100 species. This number falls as one travels north and west, particularly to the islands. Thus Ireland has only 815 species and the Isle of Man 576.

In Scotland two important lines divide the country into three main regions. The Southern Uplands Boundary Fault runs from Girvan to Dunbar and separates the Southern Uplands (Highest point, The Merrick, 843 metres) from the Central Lowlands. North of the Central Lowlands the great rampart of the Highland Boundary Fault runs from Helensburgh to Stonehaven, with the highest point in the Highlands Ben Nevis at 1,344 metres. The Central Lowlands are not uniformly low or flat, with ranges of volcanic hills going up to 720 metres at Ben Cleuch in the Ochils, and isolated volcanic plugs, often defensive sites for our ancestors, as in Edinburgh.

The Highlands are mainly very old hard rocks, heavily glaciated. They were never able to support a large population in comfort. The Southern Uplands are kinder, but still the rocks fail to give fertile soils and the winters are hard. The Central Lowlands are a giant rift valley, younger than the hill areas on either side, with better soils. Here is most of our good farmland and here were most of our valuable minerals. Here developed most of our trade and most of our industry, with much of the labour force migrating from the Highlands and Borders.

These lines are clear in the landscape. One can stand on the top of Arthur's Seat, in the Lowlands, and look south-east to the wall of the Lammermuirs and Moorfoots. As a youngster, I often went by train from Glasgow to Perth and on to Stonehaven and Aberdeen. We thundered along, through Strathmore and The Howe o' the Mearns with their red-brown soils derived from the Old Red Sandstone and their big, prosperous farms. Always to the left was the impressive front of the Grampians, presenting a solid deterrent to the Romans. As the main valley narrowed the train seemed to go even faster, hurtling down the twisting Cock's Neck to a temporary respite at Stonehaven. Beyond Stonehaven, to quote Groome's *Ordnance Gazetteer* of 1884: 'The landscape presents a striking contrast of picturesqueness and the most utter bleakness.' In other words, we were now in the geological Highlands.

The Artney is a biggish river which joins the Earn near Comrie in Perthshire. In February 2007 it seemed a good idea to climb three substantial hills accessible from Glenartney, two on the north side and one on the south. For Beinn Dearg (706m) it was necessary to cross the river and struggle up long, typically Central Highland wet moorland slopes. The upper reaches were knobbly and broken, with much bare rock but without any easily noted pattern nor any real climbing potential.

A few days later it was the turn of Uamh Bheag (664m), on the south side of the glen. At this stage in my career there is no time for sightseeing – every effort must be devoted to the task of defeating gravity. But as I was climbing the sharp-pointed northern spur I became alert. The slope was grassy, but became steeper, so steep that vegetation could not survive on it. I was clambering up an untidy mess of boulders and rounded

stones badly cemented together – conglomerate. I looked around and
the penny dropped. My hill and its outliers were rounded and grassy on
top. Looking north were the rugged and broken Beinn Dearg and Mor
Bheinn (640m) – the next on the agenda. Separating the two hill masses
was the long, straight and narrow-sided Glenartney. Beyond the glen,
Beinn Dearg and Mor Bheinn were at the extreme southern edges of the
Highlands, while, on Uamh Bheag, I was at the extreme northern edge
of the Central Lowlands.

In the Caledonian mountain-building period what are now the
Highlands were uplifted along a fault line. Immediately the forces of
erosion got to work, wearing away these new mountains and depositing
the debris south of the fault-line. The big boulders and stones were the first
to be dropped, the spaces between were filled with finer material, and over
time the mass consolidated to become the Old Red Sandstone conglomerate. Great lines of this run for miles along the edges of the Highlands
and Southern Uplands. For example, just south of Stonehaven, at Downie
Point, the headland consists of 180 metres of Lower Old Red Sandstone
conglomerate which, on examination, proves to be composed of boulders
of Highland origin. As the Old Red Sandstone period continued, so did
the erosion. The particles deposited were finer and the result was great
masses of layered sandstone on top of the conglomerate – hence the
description of the latter as the basal conglomerate.

The River Artney can now be seen as following exactly the line of
the Highland Boundary Fault. When formed, this would have been a
narrow zone of shattered and twisted rocks, more easily worn away by
ice and river action than the solid masses on either side. Even after 400
million years adjustment along the fault line is still taking place. Just
outside Comrie was built, in 1874, the Earthquake House, one of the
first purpose-built seismic stations in the western world. Earthquakes –
minor – are regularly recorded here.

Another great physical line in the landscape and on the map is the
Great Glen Fault, separating the North-West Highlands from the
Grampians and forming the Great Glen, like the slash of a giant knife
across Scotland. Long arms of the sea – the Moray Firth and the Firth
of Lorne – are joined by a long, low, mile-wide line of weakness in
which lie Lochs Ness, Oich and Lochy, linked by the Caledonian Canal.
On either side are large mountain masses. The result is a definite corridor

linking the west and east coasts but a barrier narrowing down access to the North-West Highlands from the rest – hence the strategic Hanoverian forts at the key crossings – Fort William, Fort Augustus and Fort George (better known as Inverness).

This fault is quite different from the Boundary Faults. Known as a transverse fault, a tear fault, or a transform fault, it is the result of the whole mass of north-west Scotland dragging itself horizontally along the fault line for 100km (60 miles). How can we possibly know this? One piece of evidence is that the granite rocks around Foyers, on the south-east side of Loch Ness, match those around and south of Strontian, on the north-west of Loch Linnhe. It is difficult enough to picture the vast forces at work along the Boundary Faults but can one conceive of the forces dragging around the huge raft of the north and west of Scotland? The mind grows giddy! But remember Playfair's observation at Siccar Point: 'How much further reason may sometimes go than imagination can venture to follow'.

But we are not finished yet. It has long been known that the Great Glen Fault extended beyond the Great Glen itself, along the coast of Caithness to Shetland. Now it is recognised that the Great Glen Fault is an extension of the Cabot Fault which runs from Boston, Massachusetts along the coast of New England to Newfoundland and which formed 350 million years ago, when there was no Atlantic Ocean. Could Playfair have foreseen our having to grasp the drifting continents?

We have looked at lines on a map which help us to organise our view of the restless atmosphere and of the slowly evolving, but still restless, landscape. Having them in one's mental map is a guarantee of being at ease in any company – all one has to do is to find out where one's opposite number is from to apply the mental map and come out with an intelligent comment. But we must be careful, especially with weather and climate. The Magic Quadrant is based on averages and there will be many exceptions. In fact, the weather is the mainstay of many social occasions and, for example, the Australians find it difficult to understand why, in the middle of the radio commentary on the Test Match, we go over to the studio for the Shipping Forecast. But then, as the wiseacres would say in the days of my youth: 'It's the driest spring since the year of the short corn, when the sparrows had to get down on their knees to eat it.'

Note

1 The Duke of Wellington famously said that:

> All the business of war, and indeed all the business of life, is to endeavour to find out what you don't know by what you do; that's what I call 'guessing what was at the other side of the hill'.

The submarine cable cut out the guesswork. It took information from the other side of the hill – or the mid-Atlantic – and passed it on in sufficient time for action to be taken in Western Europe.

CHAPTER 8

RLS and the God-like Sculptor

IT WAS IN CORNISH, in rural New Hampshire, that it all clicked into place. We had been in Washington DC for a week and, among all the splendid attractions of the American capital, had been struck and disturbed by the work of the sculptor Augustus Saint-Gaudens (1848–1907). Especially we found haunting and powerful his Adams Memorial of 1892, in Rock Creek Church Cemetery, commissioned by an American historian in memory of his wife who had committed suicide. (PLATE 3B) The monument was clearly influenced by both Eastern and Western cultures and the seated figure combines female and male characteristics as it meditates in what has been called 'the acceptance, intellectually, of the inevitable'.

FIG. 9 The Saint-Gaudens National Historic Site.

So now we were at the Saint-Gaudens National Historic Site, where the sculptor had had his summer home from 1885 to 1897 and lived permanently from 1900 till his death in 1907. We saw the house – an 18th century inn called Huggins Folly – adapted, extended and re-named Aspet after his father's birthplace. We saw the studio. We enjoyed the garden. We learned about the famous people and events Saint-Gaudens had immortalised.

On the way out we let slip the information that we were from Scotland. 'Scotland?' said the ranger, clad in the same Boy Scout uniform that the US National Parks Service wear whether in the Sierra Nevada, Death Valley or a sculptor's studio, 'Scotland?

Saint-Gaudens did some work in Scotland.' Producing a big book, the ranger worked his way through until he said, 'Dublin? No, that's Ireland.' But I had been reading the book upside down and was able to point out that there was an entry for Edinburgh, Scotland. 'Yes, the Robert Louis Stevenson Memorial in the Church of St Giles, Edinburgh. Do you know where that is?'

Submerged memories began to float to the surface. Yes, I had seen the Stevenson memorial plaque, wasn't there some minor scandal about it?

Stevenson, of course, was the ultimate Romantic hero. Weedy and sickly, yet writing about the active, outdoor life. Tormented by childhood nightmares, always on the move in search of health. Tense family relationships, an ambiguous marriage yet followed halfway across the world by his mother.

But how did one of Scotland's most loyal sons, who wrote so heartbreakingly from Samoa of the 'hills of home' and the wind blowing over the graves of the martyrs, come to have his memory kept alive in Edinburgh by an American, however famous Saint-Gaudens might be in his own country? Furthermore, there are two images of Stevenson generally considered to capture the essential man, the Saint-Gaudens' plaques and Sargent's portrait, painted at Skerryvore, Bournemouth in 1885. How did it happen that it was Americans who caught so successfully Stevenson's image?

Augustus Saint-Gaudens was born to a French father and Irish mother in Dublin in 1848. The family emigrated to New York when Augustus was six months old. After leaving school at 13, Augustus trained as and became a cameo-cutter, studying art in the evenings. In 1867 he was helped to go to the Paris Exposition and stayed in France till 1875, studying while supporting himself through his craft. Paris was crucial to his artistic development and most of his work was cast there. He returned to Paris from 1896 to 1900 to establish himself beyond the American scene.

After the Civil War many major American cities were establishing themselves as centres of commerce and culture. Saint-Gaudens was fortunate to be commissioned at 28 to do a statue of Admiral Farragut, the Civil War hero, and quickly acquired a high reputation. Commissions for heroic subjects rolled in. On one of the 18 occasions when General Sherman sat for Saint-Gaudens, Stevenson was present and was mistaken by the now-ageing general for one of his 'boys' who had spread devastation as they were 'Marching Through Georgia'. Although based in New York, the sculptor's summer home near Cornish, New Hampshire became the centre for a colony of artists who worked hard and played hard. On his land Saint-Gaudens had a nine-hole golf course for the summer and had a toboggan slope built for the winter. In July 1900, malignant colon cancer was diagnosed and after two major operations all his work was concentrated at Cornish where, in essence, he became the director of an atelier. He died at Cornish in 1907. He was therefore two years older than Stevenson and survived him by 13 years.

A handsome man, he was said to resemble Zeus or a weary lion, with grey eyes and red hair. In a letter to Sidney Colvin[1], Stevenson called Saint-Gaudens 'one of the handsomest and nicest fellows I have seen' – although, later in the same letter, he was to qualify this:

> I withdraw calling him handsome; he is not quite that, his eyes are too near together; he is only remarkable looking, and like an Italian *cinquecento* medallion; I have begged him to make a medallion of himself and give me a copy.

Like Stevenson, 'I will not take up the sentence in which I was wandering so long, but begin fresh'. Stevenson, having already travelled extensively in Britain and on the Continent, and having already written about his experiences, was twice in New York. In 1879 he spent the night of 18 August there on his traumatic journey from Greenock to California, to meet Fanny Osbourne again, to whom he was to be married the following year. Interestingly, in Edinburgh's Writers' Museum (Lady Stair's House), a sketch by Belle, Fanny's daughter, shows the ailing Stevenson in an upper bunk at Silverado in his characteristic semi-reclining working pose. Paper is held on his knees, with a cigarette (or is it a pen?) in his right hand. Joe Strong, who secretly married Belle, provided a similar woodcut frontispiece for *The Silverado Squatters*.

By the time of his second visit to New York in 1887, RLS had written *Jekyll and Hyde*, *Kidnapped*, *Treasure Island* and much besides. He was successful and well-known but was still searching for health. In August his little family, consisting of himself, his mother, wife and two step-children, sailed for the United States. Furnas shows us how different the American public had become. In 1879 Stevenson had been 'snubbed by editors' office boys as well as by shipping agents, railway employees and hotel clerks'. Eight years later he was: 'cockered up in luxurious hotels, solicitously entertained by millionaires, and offered private railway carriages'.

Stevenson spent a long, hard winter, mainly in upstate New York, where Dr EL Trudeau, a pioneer in tuberculosis research and treatment, reassured him by being unable to find any active disease in him. Meanwhile Fanny went on ahead to California.

Will H Low was an American artist who had become friendly with Stevenson and Fanny when they were living at Grez, near Fontainebleau in 1877. Scarcely had Stevenson arrived in New York before Low ('my old and admirable friend, Will Low') had him sitting for Saint-Gaudens. The easel was set up by the invalid's bedside, the studies began and 'it was continuously gay... as Saint-Gaudens' work grew apace'. Saint-Gaudens was a perfectionist, forever tinkering and reluctant to finish a piece ('I make seventeen statues every statue I do'). Therefore it was no surprise that he resumed working on casts of Stevenson's hands when, after winter in the Adirondacks, Low sent Stevenson to the New Jersey coast at Manasquan. The family was reunited in June 1888 and set off on a two-year cruise in the South Seas, which ended when they settled at Vailima in Samoa, where RLS was to die in 1894.

While Stevenson was cruising in the South Seas, Saint-Gaudens' work began to come to fruition. Over the next 30 years the original image was very popular but underwent many changes in shape, size and detailed design. Although all casts from the original were unique there did tend to be a succession of versions. The first version was a low-relief rectangular plaque with Stevenson working semi-recumbently with a smoking cigarette. Top left is a poem dedicated to Will H Low, reproduced below.

Youth now flees on feathered foot.
Faint and fainter sounds the flute,
Rarer songs of gods; and still
Somewhere on the sunny hill,
Or along the winding stream,
Through the willows flits a dream;
Flits, but shows a smiling face,
Flees, but with so quaint a grace,
None can choose to stay at home,
All must follow, all must roam.

This is unborn beauty: she
Now in air floats high and free,
Takes the sun and breaks the blue;-
Late with stooping pinion flew
Raking hedgerow trees, and wet
Her wing in silver streams, and set
Shining foot on temple roof:
Now again she flies aloof,
Coasting mountain clouds and kiss't
By the evening's amethyst.

In wet wood and miry lane,
Still we pant and pound in vain;
Still with leaden foot we chase
Waning pinion, fainting face;
Still with grey hair we stumble on.
Till, behold, the vision gone!
Where hath fleeting beauty led?
To the doorway of the dead.
Life is over, life was gay:
We have come the primrose way.

Five original castings and three reductions were made of this version and from the latter we can see the dedication: 'To Robert Louis Stevenson from his friend Saint-Gaudens, New York, September 1887'.

John H Dryfhout is the Superintendent and Chief Curator of the Saint-Gaudens National Historic Site and the authority on his work. He has to admit that the dimensions of this plaque are unknown, presumably because of the erosion of time. There was a major fire at the studio in 1904, but casts and moulds of other versions survived and were used for later reconstructions.

Version 2 was a large bronze medallion 36 inches in diameter. (PLATE 4A) Although Saint-Gaudens considered the circular form poor and lazy in conception he still adopted it in 1890 and used it for other versions of smaller size. Stevenson himself was cropped to fit the circle and the border and verses were re-arranged. The first casting of four medallions was in 1890 as narrated below, but this medallion began the serialisation of editions of Saint-Gaudens' work. Only a few were sold before 1900 but marketing through Tiffany in New York and Paris was successful. Dryfhout, in *The Work of Augustus Saint-Gaudens*, 1982, lists some 60 versions of the medallion extant today, which is some measure of its popularity and Saint-Gaudens' commercial success. Saint-Gaudens was equivocal about his serialisation. On the one hand, he regretted that 'a certain something is lost in the repetition'. On the other, repetition helped to compensate for the inordinate delays and extraordinary costs resulting from the innumerable changes inherent to his working methods.

Samoa in Stevenson's time was a curious place in rapid transition. It was remote, tropical, unspoiled, with lovable friendly people. Yet it was undergoing European and American colonisation, one benefit of which was a regular and reliable postal system. A result of this was that Stevenson could keep in regular contact with a wide circle of friends and fellow-writers from his tropical paradise. Thus, on 29 May 1893, Stevenson headed a letter 'My Dear God-like Sculptor' and proceeded 'to insinuate a few commissions'. Briefly he ordered:

> a couple of copies of my medallion, as gilt-edged and high-toned as it is possible to make them.

One was for Vailima, the other to be sent directly to Sidney Colvin in London. At much greater length he specified a set of two or three hundred gold letters for the house, including commas for the Samoan language.

It is an interesting comment on the efficiency of the mails, of the sea and rail transport systems, and of Saint-Gaudens' studio, that the medallion was chuckling in the warehouse of a German firm in Apia, capital of Samoa, by September 1893.

It is an equally interesting comment on the state of the roads and availability of transport in Samoa that the medallion was to sit in the warehouse until July of the next year. Amusingly, RLS outlined the difficulties – 'boys' backs' (the backs of native Samoans) were not strong enough, with only one medallion it could not be carried in a pannier and he did not have the heart to put it on the horse's back.

On 8 July 1894, Stevenson wrote triumphantly to record that the medallion had arrived and was now over his smoking-room mantelpiece. But his enjoyment of the panel did not last long. As we know, he was to die on 3 December 1894. There is an ironic symmetry to the Medallion Incident: ordering the medallion – four months, medallion lying in store – 9/10 months, medallion in place – less than four months.

Although we still think of the South Sea Islands as remote and exotic,

Adams, of the Adams Memorial with which we started off, visited the Stevenson ménage in Samoa in 1890, while they were settling down and Adams was trying to forget the death of his wife. At this date both would have had a common acquaintanceship with Saint-Gaudens. Adams was a discourteous guest and highly critical – 'poor Stevenson can't talk and write too', with 'Scotch eccentricities and barbarisms'. Fanny was 'like a half-breed Mexican'. With Adams was John La Farge, who painted and was 'friend and mentor' of Saint-Gaudens. An opportunity missed, one feels, as one party was too bohemian, and the other too strait-laced, for each to get the best out of the other. To complete the Henry Adams link, in 1904 Saint-Gaudens made a five-inch (12.4 cm) bronze medallion caricaturing Adams, whom he called 'Porcupinus Poeticus'. 'Outward gruffness and inner gentleness' were said to have been his characteristics in his later, mellowing, years.

Back in Edinburgh, the local and literary circles realised their great loss and moves began to consider how the life of Stevenson might be recognised. On 10 December 1896 a public meeting was held in the Music Hall and an Executive Committee appointed. Among those present were Sidney Colvin and James Barrie, Kipling, Meredith and Henley – RLS's old friend and sparring partner. Mrs Stevenson, the poet's mother, sat modestly among the audience until she was noticed and brought up on to the platform. The Executive Committee included Barrie and Arthur Conan Doyle. While it was considered that the best memorial would be his works it was agreed that Saint-Gaudens be commissioned to design and cast a memorial tablet based on the 1887/88 medallions he had already made.

At the unveiling ceremony in 1904, Sidney Colvin pointed out that Saint-Gaudens was overwhelmed with commissions for great national monuments. In the course of his work on the memorial he had undergone two of the most severe operations which it was possible for a human being to undergo and survive at that time. And he was also afflicted with an artistic conscience so scrupulous and so sensitive that twice or thrice the work had to be done over again. Colvin rationalised the delay by saying that it had given time for the reputation of RLS to be assured.

The committee might have been warned by the fact that Saint-Gaudens had laboured for over a decade on each of two of his finest works – the Shaw Memorial in Boston and the Sherman Monument in New York. The cornerstone for the Parnell Monument in Dublin was laid in October 1899 but the monument was not unveiled until 1911. The first Stevenson model was cast in Paris and found unacceptable by the sculptor. A new model was prepared in Cornish and cast again in Paris - and was still unsatisfactory. After more changes, the final version was selectively cast at Cornish, to find its way at last to St Giles'.

The St Giles memorial is big – 7 feet 7 inches (2.31 metres) by 9 feet 1 inch (2.77 metres) – and reverts to showing the complete Stevenson in his semi-recumbent working position. The bronze is framed by a narrow strip of rouge royale marble. A garland of laurel ends with Samoan hibiscus and Scottish heather. A sailing ship is in the bottom right corner. The poem *To Will H Low* has disappeared, despite its elegiac and valedictory style, to be replaced by the positive *Stevenson's Prayer*:

> Give us grace and strength to forbear and to persevere.
> Give us courage and gaiety and the quiet mind, spare to us our friends, soften to us our enemies.
>
> Bless us, if it may be, in all our innocent endeavours.
> If it may not, give us the strength to encounter that which is to come, that we may be brave in peril, constant in tribulation, temperate in wrath, and in all changes of fortune, and down to the gates of death, loyal and loving to one another.

On the plinth below is a summary of Stevenson's life and the signature of Saint-Gaudens, 1888–1902.[2]

Here also is the famous *Requiem*:

> Under the wide and starry sky
> Dig the grave and let me lie.
> Glad did I live and gladly die,
> And I laid me down with a will.
>
> This be the verse you grave for me:
> 'Here he lies where he longed to be;
> Home is the sailor, home from the sea,
> And the hunter home from the hill.'

The first model used instead:

> Bright is the ring of words

When the right man rings them,
Fair the fall of songs
When the singer sings them.
Still they are carolled and said –
On wings they are carried –
After the singer is dead
And the maker buried.

In what might be called Version 3 Stevenson himself is working on a couch, with more pillows than in the previous versions. Sheets of paper are scattered on the floor. He is covered by a rug and has a quill pen in his hand. The writer is at work. At some point it must have become clear that Stevenson's characteristic posture in bed, cigarette in hand, just would not do for the High Kirk or for the douce burghers of Edinburgh, however celebrated the subject might have been. So the cigarette became a pen and the unco guid were appeased, no doubt bringing a wry smile to the shade of RLS! Sidney Colvin supported Stevenson valiantly in his lifetime and did as much as anyone to promote him after his tragically early death. I would suggest that, if any one person was responsible for this rather pathetic distortion of reality, it was probably he, acting from a genuine, perhaps misplaced, desire to show off the man at his best.

The press account stated that the unveiling on Monday 27 June 1904 took place before 'a large gathering of ladies and gentlemen, which included numerous representatives of the Stevenson family'. Present also was 'Cummy', Robert's former nurse, who was about to enjoy a late flowering as the fount of reminiscence about the author (RLS's mother having died in 1897). The list of apologies was a roll-call of the best of English literature at the start of the new century – James Barrie, Edmund Gosse, Andrew Lang, Stanley Weyman, Anthony Hope Hawkins (of *The Prisoner of Zenda*), Arthur Quiller-Couch[3], George Meredith, Thomas Hardy, AW Pinero, Conan Doyle (now Sir Arthur), Robert Bridges, Dr John Watson (not the sturdy colleague of Sherlock Holmes but the Kailyard writer who used the pseudonym 'Ian Maclaren').

Lord Rosebery pointed out that the true and permanent memorial to Stevenson would be in the writers to follow him and the readers – almost idolators – of his works throughout the world. But the plaque itself was the rarest of all achievements, the memorial of a man of genius by a man of genius.

Sidney Colvin described Saint-Gaudens' difficulties in bringing his work to a conclusion but was able to demonstrate for all present the close relationship between sculptor and subject, so that the commission had become a labour of love and of deep sympathy.

Saint-Gaudens had expressed his intention of coming to Edinburgh for the unveiling, but this was quite out of the question by the summer of 1904. The 'man of genius' was never able to see for himself his memorial in its place in the church, city and hills made famous by the other man of genius. But from what we have seen, this was not just another civic commission for another Mid-West city but a resonant symbol of a short but electric friendship which survived despite the oceans separating RLS and the God-like Sculptor.

Notes

1   Colvin was Slade Professor at Cambridge and (later) Keeper of Prints and Drawings at the British Museum. He and his wife were loyal friends to Stevenson, in his lifetime and after, although later critics have attacked Colvin's influence in sanitising RLS after the latter's death.
2   In his otherwise magisterial work on Saint-Gaudens, Dryfout has allowed a misprint of the Roman numerals, suggesting that Saint-Gaudens laboured from 1888 until 1802.
3   St Ives had been left unfinished at Stevenson's death. Quiller-Couch completed the novel by writing the last six chapters.

CHAPTER 9

A Problem Solved

THIS EPISODE IS REALLY the story of a quest, of a random thought that germinated and rankled until it became vital that it be pursued and an answer found. The quest started in Edinburgh, in the National Gallery of Scotland, and took me to London, to Dresden, to Vienna, to Madrid and to The Netherlands. In the three great Dutch cities, Amsterdam, Rotterdam and The Hague, I inspected more evidence and in the Frans Hals Museum in Haarlem I found a resolution to the problem, which prompted me to further action.

Despite its poverty, its remoteness and its small size, our country has made substantial contributions to the culture and entertainment of nations. We have Scotch whisky, *Auld Lang Syne* and the 'Scotch snap' in music. We have a string of Nobel prizewinners in science and medicine. Our greatest writers have generated dozens of copies and pastiches in all the media. Above all, Scotland is the 'Home of Golf'.

But is it? Where and when did golf originate? In 1982 Steven van Hengel proved – to the satisfaction of most – that a game called *colf* was played in a number of towns in the Low Countries at the end of the 13th century. A wooden ball was struck over a set course towards a target, usually a door; sometimes the game was played on ice. From 1360 there is evidence that town officials found the game anti-social and it was banished beyond the town walls, although a variant was played indoors, in a special court. This was called *kolf*.

A healthy trade has long existed between Scotland and the Low Countries, and Dutch and Flemish records show the prevalence of *colf* or *kolf* from an early date. They show also the export of leather golf balls to Scotland, and the import of wooden clubs ('Scotch cleeks') made in Scotland. For me, this reciprocal trade between the two countries implies a roughly equal state of development, not the dependence of one country on another.

I find it difficult to accept van Hengel's assertion that the Dutch invented golf and that the game was imported into Scotland from the

Low Countries. This may only be narrow patriotism. When I was quite young I picked up that the Lewisian gneiss of north-west Scotland was the oldest rock in the world. I found great pride in this, that our poor little country should be first in something. Then the geologists got to work and found older rocks in southern Africa, then in Canada, so that our Lewisian gneiss is now only one among the oldest rocks of the world. I felt cheated. My country had been somehow diminished. This was silly, since we are considering events that took place millions of years before there was life on our planet, long before the British Isles, to say nothing of Scotland.

For all that, I still felt obliged to examine van Hengel's evidence more closely and, in particular, to wonder why golf continues to flourish in Scotland while *kolf* has long since disappeared in the Netherlands. Although survival is not a necessity for a game it is curious that *colf* or *kolf*, so well documented up to about 1700, should have quite suddenly ceased to be, just when the Scottish game was coming to the notice of travellers, writers and artists. Despite the early documentation, there is no evidence for the codification of the rules of *kolf*. In the absence of such a code, *kolf* surely cannot qualify as a proper game but remains an interesting and, no doubt, enjoyable pastime which had not enough popular support to evolve or survive. No satisfactory explanation has been found for the extinction of what had seemed to be a well-founded social activity.

One of the results of Scotland's troubled relationship with its larger neighbour in medieval times was the systematic looting and destruction of our written records, so that, while van Hengel was able to describe and quantify the development of *colf*, quoting the evidence, we just do not know, in any depth, what was happening in Scotland at the same time.

Nevertheless, there are fragments of evidence to suggest that golf was firmly embedded in our culture. The celebrated Act of the Scots Parliament of James II, in which golf and 'futeball' were banned because they interfered with archery practice on Sundays, is a measure of how deeply entrenched among the Scots people the game had become by 1457, and argues for the game having been played for a long time before then. That further legislation was needed in 1597, 1681 and 1682 merely indicates the strength of the game and the futility of trying to drive it out of the popular domain.

James IV spent much of July 1506 in and off the shores of Fife, sailing in his new warship, the *Margaret* and visiting Crail and Kinghorn. On 23 July he paid two shillings for two golf clubs, according to the Accounts of the Lord High Treasurer. They may have been used for a game at Saint Andrews. On the same day he made a payment to James Watson 'for the barnis expens in Sanctandrois' – the bairns being James's illegitimate son (aged five or six) and his friend, Watson being their tutor. Other payments were made at St Andrews on 20 and 26 July, strongly suggesting that James combined business with pleasure there, as so many have done since.

The great ones of history leave their mark in the records, but most of us just disappear like dust. James Melville was one of the little ones who left a trace. He was born in Montrose in 1566. His diary records that, from the age of six, he was taught to play different sports, including archery 'and how to use the glubb for goff'. It is suggested that this is further evidence of the deep-seated presence and popularity of golf in the east of Scotland.

The fact that golf prospered and multiplied in Scotland is in itself an argument for the early origin of golf in Scotland and its firm embedding in our social consciousness, while in The Netherlands, for whatever reason, *kolf* declined and withered away.

So much for the arguments. Was there any way I could find evidence for or against the separate development of golf and *kolf*?

A great picture tells us something about the society the artist lived in, sometimes deliberately and overtly, sometimes obliquely through the accumulation of detail. In *The Surrender of Breda* (1635), Velázquez records a moment in history and how a victor may honour a defeated enemy. In Vermeer's Delft there was at least one girl – no aristocrat – with nice regular features who could afford (or borrow?) a pearl earring. Rembrandt obviously had a cupboard full of exotic outfits he loved to dress up in for a self-portrait. An eager student could spend hours calculating the cost and time for a seamstress or an embroiderer to make a ruff and matching cuffs for one of Frans Hals' solid burghers.

Around the year 1600 a number of Dutch artists, notably Hendrick Avercamp (1585–1634) the deaf-mute of Kampen, but including also Aert van der Neer (1603/4–1677), Adrian van de Velde (of Amsterdam, 1636–72), and Adam van Breen (1585–1642), ventured into the open air to paint their fellow citizens at play. Surely the evidence I wanted could be found in their busy pictures. As a modern pilgrim, the quest began at home in Room 3 of the National Gallery of Scotland. After Edinburgh and London, I took in Dresden and Vienna and went on to The Hague, Amsterdam and Rotterdam, via Madrid. In all these cities honest Dutch burghers could be seen relaxing on the ice outside their town walls. In meticulous detail Avercamp and his contemporaries recorded crowded scenes of activity from which a great deal of absorbing and puzzling information could be accumulated.

Room 3 is not one of the spectacular rooms, full of colourful mythical heroes or buxom beauties, its riches are quiet and understated. Wealthy Dutch burghers and shipowners developed a taste for art as their prosperity increased and this is their room, of small pictures, of exquisite detail, often of ordinary scenes or objects. Two pictures in this room are relevant to our discussion at this stage. *Winter Landscape with Ice Skaters* was painted in the early 1620s by Hendrick Avercamp (1585–1634) and recognisably shows his native city of Kampen in the Netherlands. The foreground is full of the winter activities of the citizens on the ice just outside the town walls.[1]

The men are all wearing skates and a group of them are engaged in playing a game in which a ball is being struck through hoops. There is a little course with sticks and hoops, each leg being about ten yards long. (The ball is a bit of a puzzle, as any ball struck over ice will travel far and fast). There is a hole in the ice, about a foot across and with a rim round it. Avercamp crowds a great deal of activity into his picture and this hole may relate to something other than a game, like fishing.

The players are using 'clubs' rather like ice hockey sticks and they are wielded in the same way, with the right hand halfway down the handle. Is this golf? Is it *kolf*? Or is it another game entirely, a kind of target ice hockey?

Aert van der Neer's *An Evening Lowland Landscape* again shows the waterlogged Dutch landscape transformed by winter into an icy playground for nearby townsfolk. This time a group of men are holding their sticks like golf clubs and one man is driving a ball on the ice exactly as any golfer would today.

Rather than plod repetitively around half the great galleries of western Europe it would be useful to construct an Identikit *Dutch Winter*

Landscape c1600. It would have the following components:

- a frozen moat or river just outside the city walls
- a boat frozen in the ice
- the ice is crowded with small groups and individuals
- all classes represented – burghers with knicker-bockers and tall hats
- richly dressed referee or judge with an air of authority
- a group like the archery club members painted by Rembrandt and Hals gaze off to the right
- a horse pulls a sledge with a passenger in furs

FIG. 10 *Winter Landscape with Ice Skaters.* (Olrig Stephen, after Hendrick Avercamp)

- smartly dressed lady on skates, being pulled along gently by an equally well dressed gentleman
- another well dressed lady skates alone, with great dignity
- two couples on skates, women each have a broom, their voluminous skirts hide the action, one man has a club across his thighs
- a man pushes a mother and child in a kind of sledge/chair
- a man on his knees encourages a curling stone along
- various figures putting on skates, falling backwards or flat on their faces
- the village idiot sits in a little sledge/chair, chortling to himself at the failings of his betters
- a player has a woollen peasant's cap and a shapeless kind of coat
- a peg of wood, about knee-high and painted with blue and white spiral stripes, the target for one about to putt.
- a variety of clubs, some like ice-hockey sticks, some like long-nosed golf clubs, and,
- a variety of grips (beautifully observed)

- one man (poor?) has a shorter club with a crude lumpish head. Cut from a hedgerow?
- a range of dangerous or unconventional practices – a poorly dressed man is about to drive straight at a young lad – a smart young man is about to drive at the artist – a gentleman is about to injure another golfer – a solo golfer is about to strike his ball into a melee of skaters
- a man about to chip his ball into a barrel being unloaded from a boat frozen in the ice.

Busy! Busy! Busy!

FIG. 11 *A Puzzling Detail*
(Where will the ball go?)
(Olrig Stephen, after Aert van der Neer)

Plate 1A
Monument on Coombe Hill, Bucks. (In 1941 it had been struck by lightning and was supported by scaffolding. It was then covered by camouflage netting to conceal it from German bombers.)

Plate 1B
Elbsandsteingebirge today.

Plate 2A
Cliffs in the Elbsandsteingebirge, 1822/3, by Caspar David Friedrich (Belvedere, Vienna).

Plate 2B
Hutton's Unconformity, Siccar Point.

Plate 3A
La Jonction, Geneva
(Rhône on the left, Arve
on the right).

Plate 3B
Adams Memorial, Saint-
Gaudens Historical Site.

Plate 4A
Stevenson plaque, Saint-Gaudens Historical Site.

Plate 4B
Veere – main square and town hall.

Plate 5A
'Meanwhile, the Breughels
were busy drawing'
(*Van Loon's Lives*).

Plate 5B
Les Merveilles – petroglyphs.

Plate 6A
Artillery block, Maginot Line fort, Sainte-Agnès.

Plate 6B
The outpost at Pont St Louis.

Plate 7A
Festspielhaus, Hellerau – Soviet realism.

Plate 7B
Festspielhaus, Hellerau – the original décor.

Plate 8A
La Retirada – a veteran remembers.

Plate 8B
War Memorial, Glenelg.

What can we learn from this little miscellany of paintings, to add to the records of trade and town? We see town dwellers of all classes leaving the town in winter to take the air. We see a popular game. We see it played using a variety of implements. We see it being played in some kind of competitive form – but with real anomalies. We do not see golf. How can you putt with a round ball on flat ice? And how can golf fit in to a crowd bent on enjoyment? Does this mean that the Dutch invented golf and exported it to Scotland?

When the quest ended, in the Frans Hals Museum in Haarlem – although it has no ice landscapes on display – a logical solution to some of the unanswered questions was provided.

The Frans Hals Museum was built in 1608 as the *Oudemannenhuis* – a hospice for old men. Most of the great paintings of the world have ended up far from where they were created – in great national galleries or the private collections of multi-millionaires.[2]

Haarlem is immensely satisfying because it is quite different. At one time it was thought that Frans Hals – born in 1580 or 1581, died 1666 – a very old man indeed by 17th century standards and active to the end – had been one of the inmates. Not so, but he lived nearby and worked there often, painting the Governors and Governesses of the Old Men's House and similar institutions and the members of the civic militia. From 1913 it has been the Frans Hals Museum. We can now walk around the rooms where Hals worked, studying the people who ran the city and whose details are still available in the city archives. What a heritage![3]

Although Haarlem does not show Avercamp or any other golfing evidence, in a curious way this was where the writer's Dutch golfing problems were resolved for him. There is a large (five feet across) painting by Pieter Brueghel the Younger (*c.*1564–*c.*1638) of Dutch and Flemish proverbs. This is a copy of one painted by his father and both Brueghels painted a number of versions of this theme – for which there would seem to have been a big demand.

The purpose of the painting is to show viewers what they shouldn't do – and over 70 proverbs are used to get the message across. The canvas is hectic with activity, the market place is crowded, there is a river and the sea, pies grow on a roof, arrows fly around, the pigs get into the corn, and so on. I was reminded of other crowded canvasses by Dutch or Flemish painters – like Hieronymus Bosch, whose *Garden of Heavenly Delights* is packed with scores of human beings, animals (some real, some imaginary) and fantastic structures, yet so beautifully painted and skilfully arranged that every detail can be critically examined.

It then became clear to me that Avercamp and his contemporaries had been supremely competent at doing two things at the same time. They were continuing the tradition of the busy canvas, of the picture crammed with activity and with interesting detail. At the same time they were recording the everyday leisure life of a Dutch winter. People sledged, so they put in sledges. They skated – so skaters went in. People played with sticks on the ice. So they went in, too. A familiar modern technique is to take a mass of photographs, trim and arrange them to make a big composition. Avercamp was doing something similar, fitting little groups and individuals into the frame provided by the town, its walls and the moat.

I am convinced that his detailed observation of individuals and groups is as near perfect as possible. Thus we have the textbook drives, the putts and so on. But when all these activities were transferred to canvas it becomes clear that the scale cannot be correct. People may have hit balls across the ice and putted at targets – but not when others were crowding the ice. Control of the ball is quite impossible on ice – and it is futile to trot out the old defence that 'it is the same for everybody.' Boats frozen in the ice may have unloaded barrels – but golfers, or *kolfers* – did not chip balls into those barrels! Nor did they drive ferociously at innocent skaters a few yards off!

The object of this quest was to find evidence for or against the supposition that golf originated in The Netherlands and was exported to Scotland. No pictures were found of a game being played over the Dutch sand dunes, of which there are many miles. A game with sticks and balls was being played on frozen rivers and moats outside the walls of towns – but by no stretch of the imagination could this be called golf. There was evidence of some kind of etiquette, but no sign of rules. For example, sometimes the target was a hole in the ice, sometimes a short stake, occasionally painted.

Despite Sir Walter Scott[4], I consider one of the finest glories of ths Scottish legal system to be the 'not proven' verdict. In England a person is either 'Guilty' or 'Not Guilty' – which is patent nonsense when one considers how many cases collapse because of procedural errors or tainted evidence. In Scotland we are more honest. Guilty is guilty. Not guilty is what it says, while 'Not Proven' tells the truth – the prosecution have failed to prove their case. How often do we read the headline: 'Suspected killer walks free' because the press cannot bring themselves to report the 'bastard verdict'. If three possible verdicts are too many to comprehend then the verdicts should be Guilty and Not Proven. But there is little chance that the Scottish tail could wag the English dog.

With respect to the charge of Dutch invention of golf, I have to recommend a verdict of 'Not Proven', with a recommendation that there be a more thorough search for evidence either way.

My own view is that the game we now call golf was a spontaneous development of the universal 'stick and target' activity on the East Coast of Scotland, where coastal dunes and rabbit holes early framed a game based on a variety of terrain and a series of holes as targets. Neither of these was a feature of *colf* or *kolf*. Other 'stick and target' games were knurr and spell in northern England, *hornussen*, still spectacularly played in the Alpine meadows of Switzerland and *choule*, now enjoying a mild revival in Belgium.

At first, the Scots game probably did not have a proper name – I believe the game played in Kirkwall is still just 'the ba' game' – but trade links ensured that Scots and Dutch knew of each other's game and the commonality of purpose and equipment. No doubt Scots borrowed the name of the Dutch game. (Have we not seen 'football' borrowed to give Rugby football, Association football, American, Australian, Gaelic, each with its own rules in its own country?)

That the name of the Scottish game became 'golf' is not evidence that the game originated elsewhere.

Like so many of the random thoughts followed up here, answering one question merely leads on to the setting of another. Having disproved to my own satisfaction Steven van Hengel's claim that the Dutch invented golf I must now enter into the arena of controversy and prepare a campaign of enlightenment for the rest of the world.

Notes

1 In the 17th century winters in Western Europe were harder than they are now, and even now, winters in The Netherlands are colder than in Scotland.

2 Seen on a T-shirt in Los Angeles – 'In his lifetime Rembrandt painted 500 pictures – and a thousand of them are in California'.

3 The travels of great works of art – where they were created, where they are now and how they got there – is a huge and fascinating topic, which has been touched upon in many books and films. The Frans Hals Museum is quite exceptional in having dozens of pictures which were painted there four centuries ago and have stayed there ever since.

In the course of this project I came across another way of building up a great national collection. The Kunsthistorisches Museum (KHM) on the Ringstrasse in Vienna is a veritable Ali Baba's cavern of treasures – although its contribution to my golfing project (a little *Winter Landscape* by Avercamp, painted around 1605) was tucked away in a small back room.

The KHM is quite vast, yet quantity comes second to quality in one of the finest collections in the world. In another of the smaller rooms there is a smallish (127x163cm) painting which gives the key to the origins of the collection and explains why my quest had led me to the KHM.

The painting is by David Teniers the Younger (1614–1690), a skilful copyist but no old master (ale-house scenes were his specialty) and is snappily entitled *Archduke Leopold Wilhelm's Galleries at Brussels, c.1650.* In the foreground we see Teniers in conversation with the Archduke, who is surrounded by his dogs and is the only person wearing a hat, as befits the second son of one Emperor and the brother of another. Above and around these main players are 50 paintings hanging on the walls and stacked on the floor. On close inspection many of them look familiar – as they should, for most of them have been seen in the last hour!

Who was Leopold Wilhelm and why is this picture so intriguing? Born in 1614, he was made Bishop of Passau and Strasbourg at the age of 11 and Bishop of Halberstadt at 14. At 25 he was appointed Supreme Commander of the Habsburg army, then engaged in what we now call the Thirty Years War. Noble birth did not guarantee military success and he was defeated, removed from office, reinstated and replaced again. After the peace of 1648 he became Governor of the Southern Provinces of The Netherlands. The Northern Provinces were Republican and Protestant and were now free of Habsburg rule, while the Southern Provinces – which became Belgium in the 19th century – remained Catholic and loyal to the Habsburg emperors.

Leopold Wilhelm was a collector on the grand scale. He owned 542 sculptures. His Italian paintings numbered 517 and of these Teniers made 244 engravings and painted at least eight pictures of the encyclopaedic kind we see here. Our Charles I, as well as being a golfer, was a patron of the arts and bought an Italian art collection. By the time it arrived in London in 1639 he was in financial trouble – remember Ship Money? – and was unable to pay for it. Eventually Parliament confiscated the paintings and was happy to have them snapped up by the Archduke.

Eight hundred and eighty-eight paintings by German and Dutch artists were acquired so that the collection balanced the religious and classical works of the Italian Renaissance with landscapes and scenes of everyday life from the Protestant north of Europe. In 1656 Leopold Wilhelm returned to Vienna, taking his collection with him. It was bequeathed to the Emperor, to form the basis of the Imperial collection, which, after the First World War, became the collection of the KHM.

4   Scott wrote in his *Journal* for 20 February 1827: 'The jury gave that bastard verdict *Not proven*. I hate that Caledonian *Medium quid* [Compromise].'

CHAPTER 10

Peeling a Dutch Onion

I FEEL MIFFED WITH Günter Grass, German winner of the Nobel Prize for Literature in 1999. For some time now I have had the above title up my sleeve, only to discover that he had the temerity to publish (in 2006) *Peeling the Onion*. Said to be an autobiography, it is nothing of the sort, but a sequence of thoughts and incidents – more random thoughts than a life story. Fortunately, his metaphorical title is faulty and critical analysis reveals that he writes about chopping up the onion, a much more rough and ready act than peeling – which is what I propose to do. As for his theft of my title, I propose to maintain a dignified silence – as he did for over 60 years about his membership of the Waffen ss.

The Dutch onion is Veere, a small town on the island of Walcheren in the province of Zeeland, in The Netherlands.

The Royal House of Stewart used foreign marriages to enhance the reputation of Scotland abroad and to assure international support against an overbearing England. James I had twin sons. The elder died young, the younger became James II at the age of six, when his father was murdered. The new king – 'James of the Fiery Face' – had six sisters. The eldest, Margaret, was married to the Dauphin of France, but died before her husband succeeded to the French throne. Isabella was married to the Duke of Brittany. Annabella, betrothed to the second son of the Duke of Savoy, was sent to Savoy, where, as a result of diplomatic pressure from the French king, the betrothal was cancelled and the unfortunate Annabella sent home to marry a Scot. Eleanor and Joanna sailed to France, only to find that their sister Margaret had just died. James (now aged 17) tactlessly proposed that Eleanor should marry the Dauphin, who had already proved himself neglectful of her sister. Instead, she married into the Hapsburgs, through Sigismund, Duke of Austria, and Innsbruck became her main home.

By himself marrying the niece of Philip the Good of Burgundy and daughter of the Duke of Gueldres, James II continued this pattern of using dynastic marriages to forge links with powerful allies on the mainland of

Europe. Burgundy, especially, was a great prize. Comprising Flanders, the Low Countries, the southern Netherlands and northern Belgium of today, it was the most prosperous and dynamic area of northern Europe – for example, it was from Flanders that James obtained Mons Meg and other early cannon. Based on the import of wool from many countries – including Scotland – was a great textile industry which in turn generated trading links around all of northern Europe and the Mediterranean.

James's marriage reinforced the links forged when Mary, his third sister, was married to Wolfaert van Borsselen in 1444. The groom's father was Henric, lord of Veere, Sandenburg, Flushing, Westkapelle, Domburg and Brouwershaven and admiral to Philip the Good. Wolfaert was also heir to his father's two powerful cousins. Scots could now look forward to a firm foothold on the island of Walcheren in Zeeland and this was formalised by the foundation of the Scots Staple at Veere, which guaranteed favourable treatment of Scots goods so long as these were exclusively exported to Veere.

Veere may seem only a picturesque backwater now, but for several centuries it gave access to the world's trade routes for the Scots, harassed as they were by their southern neighbour. Despite minor pinpricks, as when the Scottish ship *Copin Ring* was wrecked at Veere and its cargo plundered, the trading link set up in the 1440s served Scotland well.

If we think about these matters at all, we probably think of medieval trade as a crude, hit-or-miss affair. Yet there was considerable and effective organisation. For example, the core of Scottish armies was the *schiltrom*, the hedgehog of spearmen which opponents found difficult to break down. In 1481 the Scottish spear was standardised at 17 feet 6 inches and began to be imported in bulk from Veere.

However, my first acquaintance with Veere came, not through the study of Scottish trade history, but through reading a truly remarkable book – *Van Loon's Lives*, by Hendrik Willem van Loon.

Hendrik Willem van Loon was born in Rotterdam in 1882. From his later writings we can adduce that he found the Holland of his youth 'still suffering from the after-effects of the great Calvinistic ice age of the 16th century' – narrow and censorious, prejudiced and concerned with the niceties of religion rather than its central message. As a child he loathed the sort of 'education' which was forced upon him, and at the age of 12 he had started and discontinued a *Universal Historical Encyclopedia*. At

20 he went to America out of sheer curiosity, having begun to study English seriously only three years previously (after reading Thackeray's *Henry Esmond*). He graduated brilliantly in history at Cornell University (1905) and spent a year at Harvard; becoming a journalist and passing through the Russian Revolution of 1906–7. After five years' further study of history in Munich (PhD, 1911) he returned to America to teach in universities, but during World War 1 (when The Netherlands was neutral) he was again travelling all over Europe as a reporter. In 1921 he launched upon the world *The Story of Mankind*, in which he tried to make history picturesque. The success of this revolutionary book was phenomenal; it was translated into 14 languages, and both its matter and its illustrations (all drawn by the author) aroused intense controversy. It gave the approach to history which enlightened parents and teachers had been needing. It made history live and earned van Loon the Newberry Medal.

Between the wars he continued his flow of substantial and stimulating contributions to popular understanding, interspersed with pioneer radio broadcasts and lectures for the Cunard Line. During the Second World War he broadcast to Holland from Boston and worked on his varied humanitarian concerns – refugees from Nazi persecution and war relief fund raising. He died in Old Greenwich, Connecticut, in 1944.

Van Loon's Lives was first published in 1943. It is set on the island of Walcheren, then under occupation by the Nazis, and was dedicated to Juliana (later Queen of the Netherlands) and:

> those valiant men of our beloved Zeeland who died while trying to preserve and maintain that most cherished of their possessions their LIBERTY (van Loon's capitals).

Ostensibly an interesting collection of essays on important historical figures sugared by being set, imaginatively, in the quaint old town of Veere, *Van Loon's Lives* is really a justification and a plea for liberal democracy in a world dominated by fascism.

By some alchemical process which is never spelled out it happens that historical personages – beginning with the Dutch humanist-philosopher Erasmus – are enabled to join the van Loons for dinner in Veere. Erasmus is given a little room in the old town hall and acts as go-between. This gives the book its structure as each chapter begins with a

FIG. 12
'Standing there, like Immanuel Kant, with the starry heaven above us
and the categorical imperative in our hearts'.

discussion of whom the next guests should be. Usually they arrived in carefully-chosen pairs – Descartes and Emerson, Robespierre and Torquemada, Plato and Confucius – but there were other combinations, such as St Francis, Hans Andersen and Mozart – 'but They Do Not Come Alone' (ie they brought their animal companions); the Bachs and the Breughels; the Lost Children of History; or Beethoven, Napoleon and Great-Great-Grandfather (who had followed Napoleon to Russia and ruin in 1812). 'The Greatest Inventor of All Time' – on his own – put them to considerable inconvenience.

There is lengthy discussion about the food and drink appropriate for the evening. Frits Philips, of the well-known Dutch tribe of radio and electric-bulb manufacturers in Eindhoven, did the shopping in Rotterdam and came back to Veere at the weekends. In order to brief him van Loon prepared notes on each of the guests and it is these notes that comprise the solid meat of the book. Van Loon provided the illustrations in a style reminiscent of Rembrandt's pen-and-ink sketches. Each chapter finishes with a description of how the evening went.

Van Loon's Lives was a very important book for this writer. Painlessly it opened one's eyes to a wide and liberal view of the past. Without realising it, one was acquiring a world view in which creativity and integrity were admired: bigots and megalomaniac conquerors were shown in their true colours. 'In Order not to be too One-sided... Two Members of the Feminine Sex' were invited, the Empress Theodora of Byzantium and Queen Elizabeth of England. The Buddha sent his regrets while van Loon's feelings showed since the only German speakers invited were Beethoven and Mozart. Only two of its subjects were British – refreshing for me to see how we rated in van Loon's eyes!

The last guest was Thomas Jefferson, on the eve of war:

> The clock struck twelve and we were alone with our thoughts. The noblest champion of freedom the world has ever seen was gone while the dread spectre of tyranny was rapidly descending upon earth.

For most of my life, if I had had to choose a book other than the Bible and Shakespeare to take to a desert island, *Van Loon's Lives* would certainly have been on the short leet. Unsurprisingly, a book which had made such an impression on a young teenager created in him the wish to go and see for himself. Clearly it is as much a work of the imagination as it is a straightforward retelling of history or a photographic representation of a small town. Even in one's teens one knew that many writers had created imaginary towns and even countries. How much was fiction and how much was real? What is surprising is that it took so long – over 50 years – to get to the real Veere. What would be found – if anything – when I eventually stepped off the bus? Was there still a Dutch onion to be peeled there?

I need not have worried. Despite World War II, when Walcheren was twice devastated, the Dutch have been assiduous in creating new landscapes and patching up old ones so well that they can scarcely be distinguished from the new. Van Loon called Veere:

> That delectable ruin (a veritable city and the capital of a regular marquisate), consisting of a few hundred decrepit houses, a number of gardens, and endless memories.

The Nazis invaded Walcheren in 1940 and burned its towns, Flushing, Middelburg and little Veere.

By October 1944 the Allied invasion of France and beyond was languishing as supplies had still to be carried from Normandy. The port of Antwerp had to be opened up, but even when it had been captured virtually intact on 4 September it could not be used because the Germans controlled the mouth of the Scheldt from the island of Walcheren. A long and bloody campaign was necessary to dislodge a garrison which was well-entrenched, well-armed and knew that the next of kin of those who dared to surrender would be punished. Bomber Command bombed the dykes in four places – one of them Veere – so that most of the island was flooded. Eventually, after 85 days, commandos in amphibious vehicles sailed through the gaps in the dykes and began the recapture of what remained of the island.

Appropriately, it was a lieutenant of the Royal Scots – perhaps a descendant of one of the medieval traders – who persuaded the German garrison commander to surrender. Anxious to end the battle, to surrender to such a junior officer was beneath his dignity. However, the subaltern assumed the 'local and temporary rank of lieutenant-colonel', honour was satisfied and they all lived happily thereafter.

Walcheren remained flooded for 13 months and the last gap in the walls was closed in February 1946. The flooded island was drained but the salt water had made all agriculture impossible. Of 20,000 houses on Walcheren, 3,000 had been destroyed and 12,000 seriously damaged. Ten years after the flooding the Herculean labour of reconstruction and replanting was accomplished – just in time for the next disaster, as we shall see. Yet, despite all these traumas, the Veere one sees is as trim and fresh as only a Dutch town can be.

Stepping off the bus, the first thing one sees is the *Grote Kerk*. Every Dutch town has its *Grote Kerk* and Veere's is very *Grote* indeed – far too big for its present population. In it Wolfaert van Borsselen and his Scottish bride, née Stewart, are buried. Beside the church is the *Stadsfontein* of 1551, a well with a large canopy. In Zeeland a pure water supply was a problem and in Veere rainwater from the vast roof of the church was collected and channelled into the town well, where the sheep fleeces from Scotland were washed.

In the Middle Ages the good burghers of the Low Countries towns flaunted their prosperity and defied the pancake-like landscape by building splendid lofty town halls. We used to say – 'God made the land, but the Dutch made Holland'. In Veere they made it very handsomely. The

Stadhuis of Veere, built at the peak of its prosperity in 1474, has a front garnished with the statues of the lords and ladies of Veere. A double stair leads up to the first-floor entrance. It was under one of the stone lions here that van Loon's invitations were discreetly placed and he has a sketch of the statue of Lady Anna of Borsselen, the patroness of Erasmus. Much decayed, this statue is now preserved in the Scotch House. A reminder that the Town House was the seat of justice is provided by a set of sturdy jougs. In 1594 there was added a miraculously slender belfry which now dominates landscape and seascape alike. (PLATE 4B)

FIG. 13
'Our village arising from the morning mists'.

The market place is very neat and attractive in a gentrified way, with tubs of flowers and pedestrianised cobbles. But there is enough of old Veere and a hedged green island to make one wonder whether the planners worked with their copy of *Van Loon's Lives* open at the illustrations of the Bachs and the Breughels on pages 112 and 113. (PLATES 4B and 5A)

Down by the harbour – now full of pleasure boats – are rows of 16th century houses which also functioned as warehouses. In 1561 *Het Lammetje* and *In den Struys* were built. These were the *Schotse Huizen*, the Staple of the Scottish merchants – now a museum. For me the finest feature is the superb planking of Memel pine from the Baltic, another link with the Dutch overseas trade. Van Loon showed George Washington:

> the dormitories and dining-room of the visiting skippers and business men. I told him of the strict regulations for those visitors, who were not allowed to carry the steaks they had bought at the butcher's home on the point of their swords, for that sort of thing was not done in a respectable Dutch city. They had to take them home in a bundle under their arms.

And next to the Scots' House I pointed to the house called the Ostrich, because there was a large stone with the picture of an ostrich in the façade. That is to say, people had always called it an ostrich until a professor, who knew all about birds, had happened to come to Veere and had exclaimed, 'Lord help us all if that is not a picture of a dodo!' And it was – the only image of a dodo probably ever made from an original model, brought home by a Veere sailor and done by the not very experienced hand of the local stone-cutter, but a dodo nevertheless.

We British tend to forget that the Dutch were in the imperial game very early. Indonesia was the Dutch East Indies and they were in the West Indies also. They were in India and South Africa, and Mauritius, the home of the dodo, was named after a member of the House of Orange.

Clearly there were layers of onion being found all over the place – but what of van Loon himself? His book must have been written – and illustrated – from memory in the United States. He has a sketch map of Veere in the book, with his house marked facing the harbour. But surely it would be unrealistic to expect anything tangible to have survived from the 1930s or earlier? I enquired at a fish shop, thinking that, if this were Edinburgh they would look at me oddly and send me on my way. But yes, they knew the name van Loon and yes, they were able to tell me which house he had lived in and, what is more, that there was a plaque on it. Sure enough, when I retraced my steps to the van Loon house, there was a plaque, not a very good plaque, but a palpable plaque.

In Veere, van Loon's name is not forgotten. Yet he is remembered for the oddest thing – although, when one thinks of it, it must have been typical of the man. In the 1920s, it seems van Loon became worried about the state of the fishing industry, where the big boys were taking over and the traditional boats were being driven out. As a morale booster he started races between the local fishing boats and it seems that these regattas are still part of the local calendar and have become a tourist attraction.

Next day, looking for more layers of the onion, I hired a bicycle. Cycling out of the town I wobbled my way past the ramparts constructed by Napoleon to be the launching pad for an invasion of Britain. It was Napoleon who finished off Veere as the staple and as a port of standing. (Elizabeth had sent a disastrous expedition to Walcheren. Another in 1809 got bogged down in the wet conditions, accomplished nothing and was decimated by malaria).

It was when he was out for a breath of fresh air on these ramparts that van Loon met George Washington, leaning with one hand on one of the old cannon. On the ramparts, where it could catch any breeze going, was the town's windmill. On the evening when Cervantes, Shakespeare and Moliére were guests, they were followed by their creations. Don Quixote tried to charge the windmill, then upset the local children and a chicken-woman by spearing one of her chickens, which the gallant had thought were the heads of Saracens.

FIG. 14
'The moat had baffled the noble Don ready to charge the windmill'.

My main object for the day was to see for myself how the Delta Plan had worked out. At the end of January 1953 there was a most appalling spell of weather in north-west Europe, made worse by the fact that, at that time, there was no media provision for the sharing of weather and disaster information. The British Railways car ferry, the *Princess Victoria*, was on the way from Stranraer to Larne when it was overwhelmed. Heavy seas forced open the stern gates of the car deck and the ship went down four hours later with the loss of 133 lives – including three prominent Northern Irish politicians. It was said that every household in Northern Ireland knew someone who died that night. (Even I, with no particular affiliation with the area, knew two of them.)

But in The Netherlands no-one knew of this disaster. In the southern North Sea the funnelling effect of the land, plus the wind speed around the deep depression, coincided with a high tide so that sea level reached 3–4 metres above danger level. In south-east England, Canvey Island was the worst hit. The Thames Barrier was eventually built to avert any possible repetition. In The Netherlands, the Amsterdam newspaper of

1 February (see FIG 12) underestimated the damage. In fact, 1,835 died, 72,000 lost their homes, about 700 square miles were flooded and there was a huge loss of livestock.

FIG. 15
'More than 180 dead' – front page, Amsterdam daily, 1 February 1953.

Within 14 months the Dutch had produced the Delta Plan, which would make the Zeeland area safe and alter its infrastructure for the better. Along the coast, sand dunes and a great 30km sea dyke would link up islands and peninsulas and keep out the North Sea. Behind the great dyke the existing 700km of dykes – which had failed in 1953 – would still be required, but only as backup in emergency. Behind the great dyke the enclosed water would gradually become fresh and thus available for domestic, industrial and agricultural use. Along the top of the sea dyke was built a broad fast road. Before 1953 from Rotterdam to Veere took half a day along two sides of a triangle. With the new road Veere was only 60km from Rotterdam, along one side of the triangle, with an obvious increase in accessibility in either direction.

What was the North Sea and Veere's gateway to the world has become the freshwater *Veerse Meer*, of use both for irrigation and as a boating centre. The loss of the shrimping industry has been partly compensated for by the transformation of the fishermen's cottages into holiday dwellings. One of the handsome new complexes on the north side of the *Veerse Meer* is called *Schotsman Bungalow Park*. Near the access from Veere there is a grey concrete memorial to the workers who completed the great dam here in 1961 – only eight years after the floods. Four gigantic figures are heaving on a cable in a gale.

Cycling along the dam was a pleasure, on the left hand sand dunes and seashore and trim new commuter villages, on the right polderland, fenny areas and the calm waters behind the dyke. On a windy day it could be different.

Between the islands of North Beveland and Schouwen the Eastern Schelde river used to flow into the sea. An island 5km long was created with stretches of dam at either end to close off the river. The island has commercial and leisure harbours on the eastern, freshwater, side, with sluice gates giving access to the open sea. There is a Waterland Centre with ample parking, recreational and rest facilities. Rows of wind turbines would pose a modern Don Quixote a problem of choice, but they are an uplifting sight – gentle giants conjuring power out of thin air.

The museum is splendid, with a huge model of Zeeland which fills with water in different phases, to show the floods of 1953 and the workings of the Delta Plan.

Peeling the onion was not such a good metaphor. The skins of Veere do not come off neatly and in order. There is a scrap to be seen here, another over there, another has been lost. When we strip off the layers of an onion we end up with nothing. There is no core. Veere is not like that. Veere has a core, but it is a core of the mind. This steely core enables its people to keep going in the face of adversity, to sit in the midst of their ruined lives, to get up and start pumping and draining, and to begin, doggedly, to build again for their future.

CHAPTER 11

Marvel Upon Marvel

MOST OF THESE RANDOM THOUGHTS were a long time in gestation, the passing years gradually sorting out the important from inconsequential trivia. However, it was in the 21st century that I was sitting in the sun at Villefranche-sur-Mer, just east of Nice, idly watching the hordes disembarking from the cruise liners and hurrying off to catch their trains for the fleshpots of Monaco. Flipping over some tourist brochures my eye was caught by the phrase *gravures rupestres* (rock sculptures or petroglyphs) and that there was a *Vallée des Merveilles* somewhere up in the mountains with over 100,000 of these carvings. Also there was a special *Train des Merveilles* which gave access to the three main locations of the carvings. Clearly, this was a trail to be followed. What I did not realise was that I was about to enter an area with more than two Marvels; in this corner of the Alpes-Maritimes Marvel was piled upon Marvel.

Consider a triangle whose base is the Mediterranean coast from Ventimiglia in Italy to Nice. One side would be the line of the Alps, which form the present boundary and the 'natural frontier' between Italy and France. The other would be from Nice north to the border. The recent history of this triangle is quite complicated.

In 1860 the ancient county of Nice became part of France, although some of the higher communities remained in Piedmont. (Popularly it is supposed that they were the ancestral hunting grounds of Victor Emmanuel, soon to become the first King of Italy). After unification in 1871, Italy became quite aggressive and, in 1881, started to build a chain of forts to keep out the French. A railway through the Alps from Turin to the frontier at Tende was opened in 1915. France built its own railway from Nice to Tende slowly and at enormous expense – it opened only in 1928.

Most people know of the Maginot Line, the massive fortification built from Switzerland to the Belgian border to keep out the Germans. It failed because the Germans were able to attack France through Belgium and simply avoid the Line.

France and Italy were allies in the First World War but the experience of this war and the sabre-rattling of Mussolini in the 1930s led the French government to construct 'the other Maginot Line' from Switzerland to the Mediterranean. Designed to keep out the Italians, it was quite successful. On 10 June 1940, knowing that France was on the point of collapse in the north, Italy declared war. On 14 June began the Battle of Menton and on 24 June an Armistice was signed to avoid further bloodshed. In 1943 Italy capitulated and the Germans took over, soon to do enormous damage as they retreated in 1944.

In 1947, the upper valleys of the Vésuble and the Roya were handed over to France as reparations for the damage caused in 1940 and 1944. The frontier was now – almost – the natural frontier along the watershed of the Alps. Now, with membership of the European Union, frontier restrictions have gone and all seems well.

From Nice, access to the upper Roya is by the *Train des Merveilles* which comes in two versions – one a fun and funky collection of old stock and the other a sleek, luxurious unit with a glamorous commentator fluent in three or four languages. In Britain we have become accustomed to seeing the Glenfinnan Viaduct – as in the Harry Potter films and on the Bank of Scotland £20 note – as the ultimate in railway engineering. 'You ain't seen nuthin' yet!', not until you have travelled the line to Tende.

The terrain is impossible and there are three big river valleys to be negotiated. This is done by means of over 40 bridges and almost 60 tunnels. Some of these are *hélicoïdaux* – in other words the train gains height by entering a tunnel which runs in a circle through the mountain before emerging at a higher level above the tunnel entrance. This makes for surprises and spectacular viewing, with much clicking of camera shutters. The French guide to railway tourism uses such words as 'picturesque', 'extravagant', 'unbelievable', 'uncrossable', 'vertiginous', 'audacious'.

It was very confusing to stand on the platform at St Dalmas-de-Tende, where there are two of these tunnels down-valley and one above the station, to hear a train and have no idea where it was going to emerge from the mountain, or to see one disappear – to emerge, where? All in all, the impression was of a greatly magnified model railway.

St Dalmas-de-Tende is the key to the *Vallée des Merveilles*. In Mussolini's time this was the end of the line from Turin and he had constructed an enormous grandiose station to impress visitors to Italy with his power. Today, with nearby barrack blocks and workshops, it dwarfs the village and gently moulders away. Across the road is the hotel Le Terminus, a kind of concrete rebus I found very amusing but, when I shared it with Franck, my guide, he looked puzzled. The station was, of course, the terminus of the line from Turin. But the hotel was built on an area of bare rock polished by ice and with piles of rock brought down a side valley by a glacier that ended here. This was the terminus of the glacier or terminal moraine.

Access to the *Vallée des Merveilles* is not easy and little is done to encourage mass tourism. A mountain area 7km by 2km, whose lowest point is about 2,000 metres (6,600 feet), is designated the Protected Area of the Marvels and of Fontanalba. Only 4x4 vehicles are allowed up to the refuge, which is the base for exploration. Even so the 9km trail is terrifying. For the faint of heart, from the public road to the refuge and back is a walk of 5–6 hours. Some of the named carvings are shown on the map. These have a warden nearby, during the season, to make sure all is kept in order. One big block with carvings is in the Tende museum. A replica was taken in by helicopter and fitted into the correct location. (PLATE 6A) Otherwise all carvings remain where they were cut. Sticks with metal points are not allowed, for obvious reasons.

Having said that, there are other good reasons for having a guide. Apart from a few boards at the refuge there are no signs or numbered posts. There is a main trail but the carvings are scattered about and are not very conspicuous. (PLATE 5B) Although by the end of the day one has learned to spot from a distance which rocks are likely to have petroglyphs, one could spend a lot of time searching without achieving very much.

The valley itself would be worth visiting for the scenery alone. There are spectacular peaks and rocky ridges. It shows every sign of heavy mountain glaciation – lochs and corries, ice-moulded rocks and the striations caused by moving ice. At the head of the valley is Mont Bego (2,872 metres, 9,477 feet), not high by Alpine standards but a big, tough mountain which one could believe to have daunted early man. At the *Lac des Merveilles* I thought: 'This is just like Coire a'Ghrundda in the Cuillins,' then thought – 'Nonsense.' Then I thought a little more, remembering that the uplift of the Alps began in Tertiary times. Most of Scotland is far older than that, but there was great volcanic activity in Tertiary times from Antrim (the Giant's Causeway), Mull, Skye and

Ardnamurchan to Iceland, one of the spin-offs being the Cuillins, which were later heavily glaciated – like the high Alpine valleys.

Over the day one builds up a personal portfolio of petroglyphs. In the excellent museum at Tende there is filmed reconstruction of the Stone and Bronze Age men on the slopes of Mont Bego hammering and scratching away at the smooth rock with flint tools, punching out small holes and then grinding them into lines. Some of the carvings have been given names – The Chief of the Tribe, The Christ, The Altar Rock, The Lightning Rock. The Sorcerer is sometimes called The Cosmonaut.

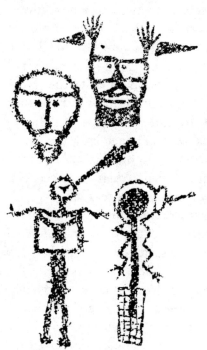

FIG. 16
Anthropomorphic petroglyphs.

The carvings fall into five main categories. The anthropomorphic ones are quite rare (0.8 per cent) and may represent divinities to be worshipped or placated. 60 per cent are 'corniform' – with horns like cattle or deer. The details vary greatly and 1.5 per cent have two or four sets of horns with added lines which might represent a yoke or, in some cases, a plough or a harrow. The horned carvings may well be associated with the cult of the bull, widespread around the Mediterranean and in the Near East. Think of the cave paintings. Think of the Israelites worshipping the golden calf (Exodus 32:1–6) and the bull-gates of Assyria. Think of contemporary bullfighting and other bull-related extravagances in Spain and Provence. Think of Picasso.

Twenty-one per cent represent the products of the Bronze Age, axes, scythes, halberds and, above all, daggers. The daggers especially are very detailed and according to size and shape, the presence or otherwise of a pommel, the number of rivets, can be compared with finds of real daggers which can be accurately dated. As well as being the tools of everyday life, there are some who think that the daggers represent the weapons of the storm god – the lightning.

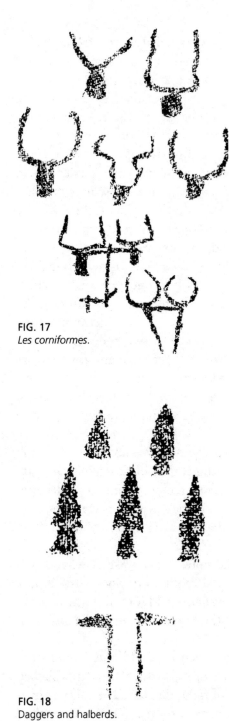

FIG. 17
Les corniformes.

FIG. 18
Daggers and halberds.

Geometric figures make up 14 per cent of the assemblage. These are circles, ovals or rectangles, very often filled with rectangles. In turn each little square may have a dot in the middle. Great puzzlement surrounds these simple figures. Are they enclosures for domestic animals? Do they symbolise land ownership? Are they field plans? Or settlement patterns? Are they isolated scratchings or do they relate to anything else?

One school of thought suggests that Mont Bego was a sacred mountain, situated at the centre of the world, where heaven meets the earth. There lived the divine couple, the bull-god and the earth-goddess. The virile god, master of the storm, breaks open the earth and fertilises it with his rain and seed. The earth-goddess takes the form of a rectangular field or a grateful supplicant with upraised hands, receiving the seed from the sky. At this height it is impossible to live all year round and those who created the engravings would have practised transhumance – bringing their flocks up in the spring, making butter and cheese in the summer and retreating to the home village in the valley below in the autumn. This is easily imagined; as a practice it is not quite dead in the Alps and it is not

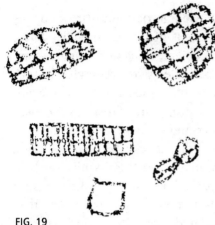

FIG. 19
Geometric figures.

so very different from what happened in the Highlands and Borders until recent times.

It is easy, also, to imagine the emotions of the Bronze Age people – the nights of terror as the mountain storms roared and the lightning struck, the anxiety as a late spring or early winter brought into question the ability of the community to feed the livestock and, by extension, themselves. In the Middle Ages it was imagined that the carvings were the work of the Devil and new carvings – some of them technically very sophisticated – were made to sanctify the locality. It was an Englishman, Clarence Bicknell, a clergyman turned botanist, who was stunned, one day in June 1881, when he 'discovered' the carvings. He had a house built nearby, at Casterino, and for 12 years searched, recorded and classified more than 14,000 new carvings, making 3,000 casts without hazarding any explanations. He died in 1918, having taken the study of the Marvels from simple curiosity to serious scientific enquiry.

The day ended with two unscheduled surprises. Franck, my guide, took me for coffee in the cabin of an interesting couple in Casterino, the base for the Marvels. She was there for the fishing and worked as a gardener in the big Riviera gardens. He was the headteacher in a special school in Monaco. It comes as a shock to realise that Monaco is no earthly paradise, but has its share of life's problems.

As I was being dropped off at the hotel Franck asked what I was intending to do on the Sunday. I wanted to climb to one of the Italian forts near the Col de Tende. Instead he suggested I join him – as a guest, not as a client – for a *manifestation* at the Fort Centrale on the col itself. Can a duck swim?

From 1881 six forts were built to defend the old Salt Route from Nice to Piedmont. At 1,871 metres (6,174 feet) the col was approached from the south by a road with scores of tight zig-zags. The railway goes through the mountains by means of a 7km tunnel. The modern road runs north through a 4km tunnel into Italy at Limone, location for the Winter Olympics, then zig-zags back up to the col and the fort. There an astonishing scene presented itself. Dozens of vehicles were ranked around. Although there was no power or water there were stalls with food and drink, as well as cultural and environmental information. At intervals there was a choir and instrumentalists playing traditional music. The crowd was divided into groups who proceeded to ramble off in all directions, depending on the topic.

I went with Franck, who led an Italian-speaking group around the Fort Centrale and along the Franco-Italian frontier to Fort Pernante, eight feet short of 7,000 feet. This was a splendid hill walk in brilliant sunshine, with fine peaks all around and mountain air like champagne. The forts were interesting and one marvelled at the fortitude of the garrisons who wintered here. Looking at the map, the frontier behaved very oddly in this stretch.

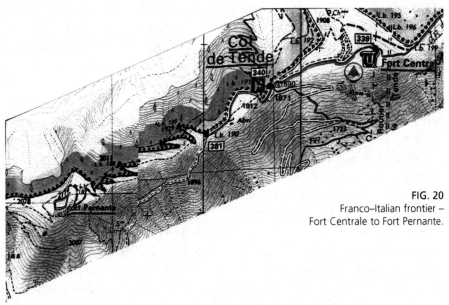

FIG. 20
Franco–Italian frontier –
Fort Centrale to Fort Pernante.

Instead of keeping to the watershed between streams running into the Roya and those running, eventually, into the Po, the border line seemed to jig about for no rhyme nor reason. On the ground, however, it became clear that a rough track followed – more or less – the crest and that, every now and then, there was a boundary marker, always on the north, or Italian, side of the road. What had happened was that in 1947, when France acquired the upper Roya communes, the new frontier was drawn so that the road servicing these high areas would be entirely within French control.

It was about this time that I became aware of some grumbling and whining in the ranks. It seemed that the Italians were unhappy about the 1947 settlement, that the plebiscite had been rigged and, anyway, many of the young men had not yet returned to their homes. Despite the fact that both countries are in the EU, that there are no border controls, that they have a common currency and live under EU law, there is still unrest. (As an example Franck's mother, born in Italy, at Tende, is now French and speaks only Italian. Franck is French, born at Tende. His maternal language is Italian, but he is equally fluent in French.)

By now Franck was getting fidgety and when we got back to Fort Centrale it was clear he wanted to be off – and fast. He had a party waiting at Casterino – did I want to come along? And so began the most terrifying experience of my life. When the Italians had these forts they built a network of rough roads linking them. Unfortunately, their transport vehicles were quite small, so the roads are narrow, loose surfaced and in decay. They are unfenced and have dozens of hairpin bends and blind corners. Always there is a 2,000 foot drop on the passenger side. Franck was already late and in a hurry when a ranger on a bicycle stopped him, berating him for irresponsible driving. Franck argued that he was late for his clients, which raised the temperature further. The result was that we were released even later and Franck drove even faster.

Saturday had been a day of high seriousness, of the Sublime; Sunday afternoon was in danger of developing into farce. Arriving at Casterino it became clear that the excursion to Fontanalba would comprise two 4x4 vehicles with driver/guides, one extended Italian family – and me. Father was tall, thin and aristocratic-looking. Laid back, he smoked little cigarillos all the time and took no part in family life. His wife was small, pretty and looked far too young to be the mother of four boys – but she was. She also took no part in family life. The four boys – one was what we called in my young days 'nae richt' – went in the other vehicle with Grandpa, Grandma coming with us.

Off we set, up a track which would have seemed horrendous yesterday but after the morning was merely tiresome. The boys were in the first

vehicle, which was open-topped. They kept walkers and wildlife entertained by howling and screaming and hanging over the sides. Arriving
at Fontanalba, we all debussed – without comment – whereupon the
unfortunate youngest began to howl, refusing to take a single step
forward. After Grandma's persuasion we all proceeded to the major set
of carvings in this valley.

Fontanalba is on the other side of Mont Bego and only 3km from
the upper *Vallée des Merveilles* where I had been yesterday, yet it is quite
different. Yesterday had been bare, rocky and rugged, with long, narrow
glacial lakes. Today we were in a big basin with a goodly number of larches.
The lakes tended to be round and shallow. They were clearly the vestiges of
a much larger lake which had almost been filled with silt and peat.

The rock carvings here are much thinner on the ground, but there is
one spectacular assemblage – *La Voie Sacrée*. A great plane of polished
rock – perhaps 10 metres across – runs downhill for about 300 metres.
Although there is nothing unusual about the carvings, it is as if all the
carvings of an entire hillside on the other side of Mont Bego had been
concentrated into this one belt of rock. A steep rocky path follows the
carvings uphill, reminiscent of the Sacred Way with Stations of the
Cross, common in many French villages. *La Voie Sacrée* was also the
ironic nickname for the road from Paris to the killing fields of Verdun
in the First World War.

Just as Franck was expounding the meaning of the rocks Grandpa
let out a howl and began running up the hill, stumbling and tripping
over the rough surface. He did himself no damage and was brought to
a halt, panting heavily. All joined in to get him back to base, where the
long descent to Casterino began. So full of the *joie de vivre* was our driver
that he chose to overtake Franck by the simple tactic of powering
through the forest, cutting off one of the zig-zags.

Monday was a very necessary rest and recuperation day. Train up to
Tende in the morning; go round the marvellous museum and then walk
back to St Dalmas-de-Tende by the High Route; taking in a 1937 Italian
fort, built to protect the station at St Dalmas-de-Tende, on the way. It
was now time to move back down to the coast at Ventimiglia by a
railway only a little less spectacular than the *Train des Merveilles* and on
to Menton, for some 20th century marvels.

Sainte-Agnès is another wonderful example of sequent occupance, of a place which has been used over and over again over several major periods of time. Said to be the highest littoral village in Europe, at 750 metres it is only 3km from the sea, a wonderful point of vantage and impossible to conquer. Post-holes of Bronze Age settlements have been found. The Ligurians had a fort here, which was taken over by the Romans, who built a road along the coast. An eighth century castle protected a church and a village, which was rebuilt every few generations in the latest style up to the 14th century. Its present state includes the most delicious and improbable garden one is likely to see anywhere.

The gardens of the Riviera are rightly famous but at Sainte-Agnès there is virtually no level ground and little but rock. Yet, in a very small space, are all the features of a great garden, formal layout, topiary, sculptures, scented garden, herb garden, kitchen garden, all hanging on the cliff-face.

Below is another great work of a more sullen description, the incredible fort of Sainte-Agnès, built by the *Commission d'Organisation des Régions Fortifiées* from 1931–34. As one of 14 major works it was part of the Fortified Sector of the Alpes-Maritimes – a southern Maginot Line to keep out the Italians. The artillery block (PLATE 6A) is a huge mass of reinforced concrete, with obvious apertures through which the guns fired, and a steel cupola protecting machine guns. What is not obvious is that this fort was like an iceberg which shows only ten per cent of its volume above water.

Sainte-Agnès was heavily-armed, with two 135mm mortars (effective in mountainous terrain), four 81mm mortars, four 75mm mortars, two twin machine guns and 14 heavy machine guns protected by steel cupolas. All could be fired by remote control and were connected electrically with each other and with the other forts. The garrison numbered 372 and the fort was like a submarine in that, if necessary, the garrison could survive underground for three months. Underground was like a small city with living and sleeping quarters. Toilet facilities for the main functions were separate, with special toilet paper ('*Utilisez CE papier*'). A little railway, with branches, was used for heavy supplies, especially ammunition, which had to be stored as far as possible from the guns. The fort had its own water supply and electricity generators. Underground, the air must have been fetid and, when the guns were firing, laden with poisonous gases – therefore there had to be a purifying plant for the inmates to be kept alive.

How many of the garrison were driven insane is anybody's guess. Certainly it is a great relief to come out into the blessed fresh air and take the old packhorse track down to the sea at Menton. Turn east and trudge along to the Pont St Louis, where France meets Italy and there was a forward outpost built to contest an invasion. (PLATE 6B) This little post had one 47mm anti-tank gun, one twin machine gun, one heavy machine gun, and an establishment of seven (although nine actually took part in the Battle of Menton).

By 4 June 1940, 338,000 Allied troops (two-thirds of them British) had been evacuated from the beaches and harbour of Dunkirk while the German armies were motoring towards Paris. This was Mussolini's opportunity and on 10 June, too avid as he was for the spoils of war to resist intervention, war was declared by Italy on France. Half an hour later French sappers began the destruction of bridges and tunnels, a task continued in turn, as the war progressed, by Italians, Germans and the Allies. On 14 June, 15,000 men of the Italian XV Army Corps tentatively began the invasion of France. An ill-equipped soldiery, spurred on by promises of a short and glorious campaign, entered a struggle which the Duce defined as being that of the 'poor and populous nations' against 'those who hold a monopoly on all the riches and gold of this earth' – Fascist empire-building disguised as the class struggle.

The Battle of Menton was fought between these so-called picked troops and, on the French side, 500 regular soldiers in the front line and 2,000 reservists in the second line. The Italians lost 866 (154 killed, 712 wounded). The French casualties were eight killed and 30 wounded, demonstrating that the French B Divisions, when properly led and prepared, could fight well and effectively.

The little post at Pont St Louis covered the only road between Italy and France and held off the Italians from 20 until 24 June, when an Armistice was declared to save further loss of life. Only when French officers intervened did the gallant little band of Pont St Louis cease firing, to find that their heroics had been in vain and that the Alpes – Maritimes were to be handed over to the enemy.

Back along the coastal boulevard at Menton is Cap Martin, where one can see – just – the most southerly of the Maginot Line forts. The Cap itself is divided up between huge *fin de siècle* villas and their gardens; and between these, in what must be one of the most valuable pieces of waste ground in the world, is a scene of dereliction. Huge concrete blockhouses lie around, askew, with corners chipped off and holes blasted in the sides. Rusted cupolas, like giant mushrooms, have been pushed over by immense forces. Having been at Sainte-Agnès we can now imagine what it must have been like for the 300 men inside. What we know is that, during the battle, the Cap Martin fort was hit by 1,500 projectiles from different sources – big guns, armoured trains and aeroplanes – 'sans aucune perte' (with no loss whatsoever).

Looking back at this triangular territory, I had been over some beautiful country and seen some amazing things. The landscapes had been very fine – the high Alps, the lakes and rivers, picturesque towns and villages, the front at Menton. Not, perhaps, beautiful, were the works of Man, the proliferation of rock carvings, the boldness of the railway builders, the ingenuity of the military engineers – but, by Jove, they were interesting. I found myself trying to look behind the façade of simple admiration, thinking of Gross Domestic Product and opportunity cost. Sainte-Agnès cost 16,821,000 francs at a time when France – and most other countries – was still suffering in the wake of the Great Depression. Some authorities suggest that it was governments spending on rearmament that pulled us out of depression. How sensible was it to spend 16 million francs on one fort which may have had some short-term military success but which, in the long sweep of history, was irrelevant and does not even rate a footnote?

Could not the money have been better spent? And on what? And why is it that we seem to be able always to spend what we cannot afford on swords and spears and not on ploughshares and pruning hooks?

The railways of the triangle had been built at a huge cost in francs, lire and lives; only to be destroyed for military reasons. What waste! It was not until 1979 that they were brought back into use.

When we consider Les Merveilles we must suppose that their creation was a long-term process and a basically peaceful one – despite the prevalence of daggers and halberds on the rocks. The permanent homes of the Bronze Age carvers were far below, by the Roya and its tributary valleys. Only from late spring to autumn did the snow of the upper slopes around Mont Bego clear away to give summer grazing for domestic animals and to expose stretches of ice-polished rock suitable for carving. How was the carving done? Did the holy men of the villages perform a summer pilgrimage from the low ground and indulge in a brief season of carving? Or did those caring for the animals on the high pastures take time off from their herding duties to perform practices that would placate the forces of nature and guarantee the survival of the tribe?

Gaelic literature is full of reference to the pleasures of summer up at the shielings; light work of milking and cheese-making and the long summer evenings, the young men and women together with the minimum of adult supervision. No doubt the Alps were little different and there would be time for some carving. If the Bronze Age people used these high pastures for 1,000 summers they could have cut 100 images in a season, or about one per summer day. Given that the carvings are not large, nor particularly well-finished, this seems a very likely work-rate, well within the capacity of a tribal community and not requiring a large labour force of slaves or devotees of the cult. Opportunity cost? What could the carvers have done with the time had they not been carving? Like the Highlanders, dancing? Singing and making poetry?

Looking back at Marvel upon Marvel, it is tempting to contrast the Bronze Age, with its apparent ability to maintain a mountain economy and have some kind of spiritual life, with our own industrial society and its associated social turmoil and flagrant waste of resources. No doubt Bronze Age man considered the effort of cutting the petroglyphs worthwhile as the gods continued to deliver enough sun and rain to keep their world going. Looking at the damage one set of men can inflict on another set in a mere five years, even in a military backwater, could be enough to make one weep.

And yet, 60 years on, the scars have healed, the ruins have been rebuilt and French and Italians cross and recross the frontier without fear. Perhaps this is another Marvel to add to the ones in the guide book.

CHAPTER 12

Hellerau – Dream Turned Nightmare

I AM INDEBTED TO my father, not only for introducing me to the two greatest socialist novels of the 20th century, but for making me aware of Upton Sinclair (1878–1968), and especially his *World's End* series. Although scarcely read today, Sinclair was an influential and popular writer in his time. His *The Jungle*, a powerful and harrowing description of the meat-packing industry in Chicago and the exploitation and degradation of the immigrant workers who kept it going, has just been re-issued by Oxford World's Classics.. Unfortunately the final pages move beyond narrative and description to an extended polemic and political statement, difficult to digest at a distance of 70 years.

Incredible as it must seem now, Sinclair came very close to being elected Governor of California in 1934, only being defeated by an unholy alliance of the big employers intimidating their employees and a vicious 'dirty tricks' campaign in the William Randolph Hearst ('Citizen Kane') newspapers.

In an author's note to *A World to Win* (1947), Sinclair in effect bade us farewell and stated his credo:

> Up to the year 1938 there had been issued in European countries a total of 690 titles of the books of Upton Sinclair, and in India, China and Japan, a total of 57. The number of books cannot be estimated, but in Britain, Germany, and the Soviet Union the total was over seven millions. I have no way of learning how many of these readers have survived the Great Blackout, but I take this opportunity to send to them my greetings and my hopes. May they succeed in building the new world, dedicated to the practice of democracy, both industrial and political, as I have tried to explain it in many books and pamphlets.

Again, in *Dragon's Teeth* (1942), he had said:

> In tragic times like these, an elderly author has nothing to give but words. This collection of words is dedicated to the men and women in many parts of the world who are giving their lives in the cause of freedom and human decency.

By 1944 Sinclair had learned how to be political without being tedious. As *The Scotsman* said: 'Mr Sinclair... is far too fine a craftsman to spoil a good story by pretentious propaganda.' *The Field* (ultra-conservative!) stated the view that: 'Mr Sinclair is a great writer – he has some claims to be considered the Tolstoy of America.' The *Manchester Guardian* took up the *War and Peace* comparison. Their reviewer said that:

> Many famous people... appear as characters in a vast canvas in comparison with which that of *War and Peace* seems almost provincial...

As a historical novelist, Sinclair is remarkable for the intimacy with a huge spectrum of the historical figures he shares with us – Hitler and Goering, Roosevelt and the peacemakers at Versailles, Clemenceau and Blum, Churchill, Zaharoff and the other arms manufacturers, even Einstein. Characteristically he nails his colours to the mast unequivocally in an Author's Note in the first of the series (*World's End*):

> In the course of this novel a number of well-known persons make their appearance, some of them living, some dead; they appear under their own names, and what is said about them is factually correct. There are other characters which are fictitious, and in these cases the author has gone out of his way to avoid seeming to point at real persons. He has given them unlikely names, and hopes that no persons bearing such names exist. But it is impossible to make sure, therefore the writer states that, if any such coincidence occurs, it is accidental. This is not the customary 'hedge clause' which the author of a *roman á clef* publishes for legal protection; it means what it says and is intended to be so taken. Various European concerns engaged in the manufacture of munitions have been named in the story, and what has been said about them is also according to the records.

A later Author's Note in *Presidential Agent* (1942) sheds more light on Sinclair's technique. He wrote:

> In the course of this work of fiction there occur several scenes with Franklin D Roosevelt. When the author was a candidate for the governorship of California he had the pleasure of a two-hour conference with President Roosevelt, but since that time he has no first-hand knowledge as to his reasons for this or that action or attitude. The scenes in this book are fictional, and neither the President nor his wife has been consulted concerning them. The description of the President's

appearance, mannerisms, and surroundings the author can certify to be accurate, but the speeches attributed to the President represent merely the author's guesses as to his mind. The author hopes they are good guesses, but does not wish anyone to assume that he speaks for the President or is in a position to reveal his secret thoughts.

Sinclair assumed a reasonably high level of literacy in his readers, for example, Book Four of *A World To Win* is headed 'Put it to the Touch', reminding us of the lines of James Graham, Marquess of Montrose:

He either fears his Fate too much,
Or his deserts are small,
Who dare not put it to the touch,
To gain or lose it all.

These are big books, 600 pages long – 'blockbusters' written when a blockbuster was still just a concrete-piercing bomb delivered by a Flying Fortress – but the interest never flags. Partly this is due to the subject – the greatest upheavals of the 20th century – partly to the interweaving of great events and famous people with the lives of an international group of friends. Forward momentum is generated by the structure of the series.

On the first reading as a teenager, sex and violence seemed to be absent. Read again years later, a hero who has a flighty mother and a string of wives and relationships of varying intensity is clearly no innocent – but no clear depiction of the messiness of sex is necessary for the mature reader. At the same time, the main character, Lanny, moves in an atmosphere of violence but generally contrives to avoid first-hand contact with blood and guts or Ian Fleming heroics. Nevertheless, as with many other great writers, the emotions are there, but concealed under the surface of a polite society – too subtle for a teenager!

World's End is the first book of the series, published in 1940. In it Book One is entitled 'God's in His Heaven'. Chapter 1 is 'Music made Visible' and it begins:

The American boy's name was Lanning Budd; people called him Lanny, an agreeable name, easy to say.

The year is 1913 and Lanny is 13 – the same age as the century – and growing fast. He is in Hellerau, in the suburbs of Dresden, at the

Festspielhaus, a tall white temple with smooth round pillars in front, and this day of the *Festspiel* is the most delightful of days.

Lanny has two friends, slightly older (thus ensuring that they can serve in the war soon to break out), while the American Lanny remains an intelligent observer. Rick is an English aristocrat with a hyphen and Kurt Meissner is the son of the comptroller-general of a great estate in Silesia. It is the latter who explains, in his pedantic German way, that 'Hellerau means bright meadow.' A cultured assembly has gathered at the Jaques-Dalcroze School and the boys are about to take part in a performance of Gluck's *Orpheus*, transformed into Eurythmics and performed by the bodies and bare arms and legs of children.

Dalcroze himself stands on the steps of the temple, surrounded by an array of celebrities, such as 'a great blond Russian named Stanislavsky.' The boys have an encounter with 'the king of celebrities', George Bernard Shaw, but all is beautifully controlled. To ask for an autograph was a crudity undreamed of in the Dalcroze school.

After the rapturously received performance Sinclair allows himself a couple of paragraphs of moralising, which form the base level for his great sweep of narrative. Everyone at Hellerau believes that humanity can be saved by beauty and grace. A new Orpheus will charm and inspire and the furies of greed and hate will be won over. In the Dalcroze school, children of the well-to-do danced with children from the factory suburbs. The spread of civilisation was automatic and irresistible. Forty-two years had passed since Europe had had a major war (although there had been a few messy campaigns in the Balkans, filling the powder keg which would be sparked off in the summer of the following year). According to

FIG. 21
Furientanz aus Orpheus.
(Dance of the Furies from Orpheus from
Das Junge Hellerau)

Sinclair: 'Love and brotherhood were stealing into the hearts of the furies.'

It is 1913. We are in a golden place and on the edge of a Golden Age. The rest of this great literary sweep uses Lanny Budd as a vehicle, or rather an agent, to show us what went wrong, and why. After the summer school Lanny returns to his mother's home on the Côte d'Azur and resumes the free-and-easy life of an expatriate American. Lanny is the love-child of an arms manufacturer who visits from time to time and involves him in travel and the arms trade as he grows older. Beauty, his mother, is part of a wealthy circle in the south of France. Cultivated and delightful, her frivolity is tempered as the war proceeds and she becomes involved with a French painter who is, first, horribly disfigured, then later furiously paints a series of works which will provide financial security for many years to come. He then returns to the front, to be ground up in the terrible mincing machine of Verdun, 10 months of the ultimate exercise in futility.

Lanny has his French base and his mother's connections – she has a brother in Paris who is a bad painter and an active Communist. His father leads him into the wider world, even taking him back to New England in 1917, where he acquires a brief formal education as a member of the Budd family. He has his Hellerau friends to visit, adding another dimension of travel and social experience.

When it becomes necessary for him to work for a living, Lanny becomes an art expert and adviser – dealer would be too coarse a word – and this provides another reason for travelling around, meeting and getting into the homes of the wealthy and high-born. It is a pleasant life – one of Sinclair's chapter headings sums it up beautifully in quoting AH Clough ('How pleasant it is to have money, heigh-ho!'). In the later books this dilettante life provides a perfect cover for intrigue and activity as a Presidential Agent.

It would be easy to despise and patronise Lanny, as does the robber-baron Göring, who nevertheless finds him useful. But Lanny has a conscience. He finds terrible poverty everywhere, behind the glittering promenades of the Riviera, in the East End at the heart of the Empire, beneath the lamps of Montmartre, in the feudal cottages of the German forests. Emphatically not a Christian, he looks for ways to help. He gets involved in some scrapes, particularly once the Fascists have taken over

Italy, Spain and Germany, and causes some apprehension in his families and his social set. Yet, while some of the poor are admirable and honest, too many of them are dirty, unattractive and threatening in their behaviour – whatever the underlying causes!

All through his life, because he is serious and thoughtful, Lanny is pulled in two directions. Born into a world of ease, he has attractive and clever friends. He is surrounded by wit and beauty. Yet he cannot totally accept this. He feels guilty that so many others are excluded from the finer things of life. 'Something must be done' said the Prince of Wales, then popped off to another cocktail party at Fort Lauderdale. Lanny tries. Sometimes he is exploited, sometimes he falls flat on his face, but he keeps on trying – and because he is rich and well-connected he usually escapes the full consequences of his actions!

In quoting so extensively from Sinclair's own words I have tried to convince the reader of his power. This whole great sweep of historical fiction clearly made a very strong impression on me. The opening scene, because of its importance in registering the high point of European culture before the descent into barbarism, became especially memorable.

For most of my life I have been interested in planned settlements, industrial villages and other attempts to create 'heavens on earth'. In Scotland I knew New Lanark when it was still a home for active industry. I grubbed around, off the beaten track, searching for the remains of textile villages made obsolete when water power was superseded by steam. In England I admired the Christian compassion and good business sense of Titus Salt at Saltaire and the splendid semi-rural creation of Port Sunlight by William Hesketh Lever, Lord Leverhulme (1851–1925).[1]

I have spoken to dozens of audiences about Ebenezer Howard, his *Three Magnets*, the Garden City ideal, Letchworth (1904) and Welwyn Garden City (1906), not forgetting the Ovaltine factory – 'the factory in the country'. The *Deutsche Werkstätte* (German Workshops) in Hellerau were founded in 1898, as an idealistic attempt to make fine German furniture and crafts using modern machinery, with designers and crafts-people living in an idyllic, purpose-built garden suburb setting based on the English model:

> The factory area and the living houses were built like a green organism: the factory was the heart, the veins formed the streets and ways, the houses were the organs and the green areas were the bones.

Prizes were won in International Exhibitions in Paris and St Louis. An artists' colony was established nearby. A Town Hall was built in 1924 and a market square in 1929. Hellerau was incorporated into Dresden in 1950. Surely Hellerau was worth a visit in its own right as a planned Utopia.

The *Festspielhaus* was built as a cultural centre in 1912, completing the founder Dohrn's dream of a total urban artwork with unity of working, living and art. It is held to have been the birthplace of modern theatre. Kafka, Diaghilev, Kokoschka, Rilke, Le Corbusier (who called it 'the laboratory of the new human being') and Rachmaninoff were among the famous visitors not mentioned by Sinclair. The event described by him took place in July 1913 and was attended by more than 5,000 visitors. AS Neill, founder and headmaster of Summerhill, started his first school in Hellerau. Dalcroze's move to Hellerau was clearly an ideological decision and not based on economic considerations. He brought 46 pupils with him from Geneva, by 1913/14 there were 495 pupils from 15 nations.

Dalcroze Eurythmics was not classical dance nor was it a soft option. Upton Sinclair saw grace and emotion, for the dancers it was strenuous, physically and mentally. The rhythm could change from 2/4 to 9/4 and the dynamics – crescendo and decrescendo – had to be matched by muscle tension changes. All at the same time, the head could be moving in 2/4 time, the left arm in 3/4, the right arm in 4/4, the legs in 5/4. And as well as coping with the physical and mental complexities the children learned to be graceful!

The First World War cut short the international bohemian flowering. (On the outbreak of war Dalcroze moved to Zurich in neutral Switzerland – another ideological decision). The progressive community came to an end in 1933. Free-thinking artists were totally unacceptable once Hitler came to power. The workshops survived, to be pressed into working for the Wehrmacht, latterly making wooden tail assemblies for planes. They may even have made wooden parts – if there were any – for the V-1s and V-2s. Under the DDR they went back on to furniture making. In 1990 they reverted to individual enterprises making luxury articles, such as the Zedernholz-Schatullen humidor for cigars, at 15,000 Euro each.

The *Festspielhaus* was taken over by the military in 1936 as a recreational facility for the ss and in 1944 it was a fortified ss barracks.

It became the headquarters of the Russian army in the Dresden area, and was a hospital and a barracks until 1992, when the Soviets left it in a very bad condition. The ying and yang symbol on the pediment was replaced with a red star. Could anything worthwhile have survived from this turmoil? Was there any point in trying?

This writer has been in Dresden four times, twice when it was part of the DDR (the former East Germany), and twice since the Wall came down, once before and once after the Flood of the Century. It could be asked why, if I was so interested in Upton Sinclair, if I was so influenced by him, it took me till the day before my 70th birthday to get to Hellerau?

When my father died I was left his books and, for the first time, became the owner of a neat little row of Sinclair's work. Over the years I had read them intermittently, as they came out and when I felt I needed refreshment. However, remembering their importance for my father and their influence on me, as an act of filial piety I began to read my way through the saga as continuously as one can in a life beset with trivialities. No penance this, armed with all I now knew about the world since 1913. I found myself driven along by the power and sheer interest of the narrative. Inevitably, Hellerau came up again as the starting point. The guide books told me that it still existed, though much decayed. How much of Lanny Budd's Hellerau still existed? Had it ever existed? Does a great writer need to reproduce faithfully every brick and tile of his settings?[2]

To answer these questions it became necessary, before it was too late, to see for oneself the supposed birth of the Lanny Budd saga at Hellerau and to establish to what extent that first chapter was a description of reality and how much was pure creativity.

Not the meanest attribute of that fine city, Dresden, that 'Florence on the Elbe', is the transport system. As well as being a major rail centre with a suburban network, there are trams and buses, steamers on the Elbe and a passenger ferry across it. There is a funicular and the world's oldest *Schwebebahn* (suspension railway), opened in 1898 and renovated in 1980.

For the geographer the number 8 tram – destination Hellerau – cuts an interesting cross-section across the city. From a southern suburb it passes the main railway station and the Stalinist city centre imposed on the ruins of 1945. It slides through the glories of the Zwinger, the Opera House, the Frauenkirche and over the Augustus Bridge to the Golden

Rider statue (Augustus the Strong, recently restored to his glory). The New Town of Dresden is full of splendid boulevards, fine buildings, parks and fountains, but as we glide northwards, away from the Elbe, the townscape deteriorates – indeed, it ceases to exist. Instead we have a zone where the housing was good a century ago but has failed to recover from war damage and half a century of misrule and neglect at the hands of the Russians and their East German subjects. Railways and marshalling yards intervene, with as much of their land unused as is in use. That huge building on the right, several stories high and about a kilometer long, was the *Heeresbäckerei*, or army bakery, where, presumably, bread for about half the German army was baked. It has found a new life as the Central Record Office for the Land (the former Kingdom) of Saxony, of which Dresden is the capital. Factories and warehouses stand derelict, but for the stranger in a tram it is impossible to apportion blame properly. Is this the long-term conclusion to the policy of bleeding the East German economy without re-investment? Or the immediate result, following re-unification, of tired industries having to face competition from the West for the first time? Or, as one suspects, both? A long, wasting, illness terminated by a swift *coup de grace*.

Till now the tram has been running along the middle of a main road, but for the last stage of the journey the line becomes single and is private, with its own ribbon of territory beside what is now a minor road. We are now in the Rural-Urban Fringe and on either side is light woodland, not the dark forest of German myth, but the kind of woodland where children cycle, young ones jog and older people walk the dog.

Descending from the tram it is obvious that this part of Hellerau is no throbbing downtown. There are a couple of modest hotels and restaurants and little else. Going along the side roads is a very rural experience, rather like getting off the main road where Berkshire, Surrey and Hampshire meet. There is little uniformity here, and certainly no grandeur. It is very much a garden suburb in that all the houses are pleasant, quite roomy and set in their own gardens. There are a few rows of six or eight houses. Like Port Sunlight, for example, they are not aggressively modern in style. Rather, they look back in what one might call a German equivalent to the Arts and Crafts style.

There is no grand approach to the *Festspielhaus,* instead one turns off the main road, passes through a modest archway and finds oneself in a large square – just like a parade ground. Three sides are made up of single-story workshops/students' dwellings in an easy traditional style. The *Festspielhaus* itself is in a clean uncluttered blend of Saxon and Bauhaus. The columns on the front are rectangular, not 'the smooth round pillars' of Upton Sinclair's memory or imagination. 'Upon a high plateau stood a tall white temple' reflects the architect's first draft rather than the building we now see. Given Sinclair's introductory remarks it must be clear that his description of the event was derived from reports and his description of the *Festspielhaus* comes from an assumption that Eurythmics and classical dancing can only be done in a classical building. If this is a temple of culture it is a modest, well-mannered temple with no extravagances.

A big hoarding announces a European Union restoration project among a few tired posters and an injunction not to enter. However, obeying the Duke of Wellington's advice to: 'push on till you're stopped, then go round', I push on and find the doors open, the place deserted and a state of semi-dereliction within.

Inside is a big hall with, at either end, a set of stairs giving access to the first floor. Beyond the hall, on the ground floor, are some big rooms of which one must be in occasional use as a concert hall as it has rows of

FIG. 22
First draft of Dalcroze School with the
Great Staircase.
(from *Das Junge Hellerau*)

chairs and the walls are camouflaged by heavy curtains. Everything else is tired, to say the least, damp and with disintegrating plasterwork. A sad sight – but there is evidence to be found!

At the top of the stairs there is an overpowering tribute to the Soviet troops who made this their headquarters. A giant heroic figure with a majestic sword is on the left, with a mighty red flag behind him. A map shows the movements of the unit, from north of Moscow to the Baltic, and on to Berlin and Dresden. There are scenes of battle and we note the Reichstag. The red star is prominent.

A balancing panel is at the top of the stairs at the other end of the building. (PLATE 7A) Another heroic figure with a monstrous sword is backed by a huge star, labelled CCCP (USSR). The campaign on the map starts and finishes at the same places, but the journey between is more direct. There is one battle scene. A female soldier is rescuing a ghastly wounded ambulance man. A field dressing station is on the left. Shells explode all around. Planes fly overhead and a disabled tank is on the right.

The message is unequivocal. I was in the presence of Soviet heroes.

Downstairs, at the back, a big room was in an advanced state of decay, with some graffiti that turned out to be much more than that. Someone had taken the trouble to paint in a poem by Brecht about a girl who was in the habit of going out at night to ply her trade, but who reassured her parents that it was safe in the moonlight. She was wrong, of course. A placard with the word 'Jew' on it was hung around her neck before she was shot for breaking the curfew.

This is a puzzle. It must be post-1945, but it is in German and one cannot see a Russian approving of the sentiments implied by Brecht.

Another puzzle is a fragment of plaster wall in a corner of the main entrance hall. (PLATE 7B) This is a real treasure, a lively scene of subversion. Dominant is an authority figure, black-caped and black-booted, but not the traditional gendarme of Paris, the *rossignol* (nightingale) who used to direct the traffic with his whistle and baton. With *kepi* and blue cape he was an attractive authority figure. This one is not. The other characters are in the Hellerau tradition of freedom and beauty. Very naked dancers skip around, a Japanese woman plays her instrument while an intellectual (Cocteau? Stravinsky?) sits smoking and thinking great thoughts. This must be a fragment of the original décor, referring to the naïve freedom and pleasure of 1913. It reminds me of Ibert's *Divertissement* of the 1920s, played at breakneck speed and ending in a cacophony of police whistles and car horns.

After the Soviets left, the *Festspielhaus* crept back into the informed consciousness and intermittent efforts were made to undo the neglect of 70 years. In 1996 it was designated one of the 100 most important endangered sites under the World Monuments Watch Programme. A grant of 250,000 dollars by the J Paul Getty Trust was only one of several initiatives which have successively turned the old crumbling temple of the arts into a fine modern theatre of 560 seats. There is now a 'walk-through' on YouTube which does just that, so that we can admire the beautiful clean lines of the reborn *Festspielhaus.*

What cannot be picked up is the fate of the murals. Was the Soviet Realism jettisoned in a fit of liberal reaction? Did the wish for clean antiseptic surfaces see the naughty dancers covered up? Was I going to have to spend a small fortune to travel to Dresden for less than five minutes of verification?

After four approaches in various media were ignored, the task was handed over to a 'private eye', Herr Wolfram Schaue. His first finding was that the *Festspielhaus* was closed, yet again, for a renovation project and would not re-open until May 2009. Well, like Mr Filmer in *A Chorus Ending,* 'a skilled old ferreter is not easily turned back, however deep the dead thing is buried' and eventually there came into my hands various booklets, annotations and, best of all, a *Festspielhaus Hellerau* calendar for 2008, which shows on the cover the first Soviet mural and for August the second in its reconstructed corner. The subversive mural will be retained after the present work is complete.

So the story has a happy ending. Hellerau started as an idealistic and optimistic inspiration but the gentle and kind people were hunted out by the jackbooted forces of militarism. However, after a long interlude, Hellerau has been reconstructed in something like its original form. Crushing conformity has been ousted. Individualism and creativity are back. Less naïve and more realistic, perhaps, but after something like a century Germany has regained an institution of which it can be proud.

By the way, what were the two Greatest Socialist Novels of the 20th Century? Remembering that this statement was made about midway through that century, it may be that this judgment is out of date and better novels have been published since. But Robert Tressell's *Ragged-Trousered Philanthropists* and Lewis Grassic Gibbon's *Sunset Song* are still remark-able books and the latter has the added distinction of being probably the best Scottish novel of the 20th century.

Notes

1 Characteristically, throughout the Second World War Unilever made up my father's Air Force pay to the salary he had had in 1940. Their loyalty to him was rewarded by his decamping to another employer immediately he was demobbed! In his defence, because of the post-war shortage of edible fats, there was no job for him at Unilever for several years.

2 I recall a heated discussion with a lady on Salisbury Crags, in Edinburgh, who wanted me to point out the actual cottage Jeanie Deans of *The Heart of Midlothian* lived in, as if a great writer like Scott needed a real example of such an everyday feature in which to embed his fictitious character.

CHAPTER 13

'Die Vergeltung kommt!'

I AM NOT OBSESSED by Dresden. Splendid city though it is, there are other beautiful cities which have had their share of interesting indwellers and dramatic events. Yet, for me, it seems to have had a peculiar kind of attraction, based, I think, on the alternation of elevated thinking and brutal destruction it has endured over the last three centuries, and more. Dresden is not unique in that respect but, for some reason, more than for Munich or Marseilles, I have wanted to go there and see for myself.

Most travellers still come to Dresden by rail from the north, so that the spires and towers of the city centre are seen in the distance until the railway sweeps round in a great curve and the vast main station is entered.

Most of those who arrive then walk down to the architectural splendours beside the Elbe. It only takes a few minutes to realise that something pretty dreadful must have happened here. The first few minutes are spent heading northwards, marching along grey Stalinist streets of multi-storeyed flats and shops, all dating from the same architectural lowpoint – the 1960s. Even a visitor from Mars would realise that a vast swathe of this city had been destroyed at one time, cleared away and rebuilt cheaply and brutally. Stone was the building material of the historic core and there is still plenty of it around – blackened and corroded worse than the inside of any railway tunnel in our country – once we get down by the river. After more than 60 years restoration is still going on. The visitor finds it difficult to imagine the horror which must have roared through the city, branding the very building stones with its heat. A big plaque in the entrance arch to the Zwinger, the city's centrepiece, records what happened on 13 February 1945.

Taylor's magisterial *Dresden: Tuesday 13 February 1945* (published 2004) describes these events. As well as being well-researched, it has the advantages of being recent and of having examined in detail many of the accusations made against the Allies in the post-war years. His survey of war in the air begins in 1911 with Italians bombing Turks. From 1915, Zeppelins regularly bombed south-east England and from May 1917 Gotha bombers attacked London by day and night.

Britain retaliated, of course. In the last six months of the Great War (as my grandfather called it) the newly-formed Royal Air Force mounted 675 strategic raids, killing 746 German soldiers and civilians at a cost of 352 aircraft and 264 aircrew. One German killed per air raid, one airman killed for only three Germans – could this be regarded as a satisfactory return on the investment?

How to explain this? Where to begin? In Paris, during the Siege of 1870–71? Where, for three weeks from 5 January, 300 or 400 shells arrived every day, at random and with no attempt to single out military targets, marking 'the beginning of the Germanic technique of war by *Schrecklichkeit*'. At least 400 Parisians were killed by the same model of Prussian gun that had been proudly displayed in the heart of the city in the great exhibition of 1867, held on the *Champ de Mars*. The bombardment outraged Europe and achieved no tangible success. When the humanitarian Crown Prince of Prussia (son-in-law of Queen Victoria) learned that shells had exploded among a church congregation, he exclaimed, 'Such a piece of news wrings my heart'.

As a simple traveller, I would start with a stained glass window in the church of Saint Gervais, in Paris. On 24 March 1918, 'Herr Krupp's little toy' opened fire from behind the German lines 110 kilometres away. A huge, long-range German gun was firing from a clearing in the forest of St Gobain near La Fère. Aimed at the Louvre, not a single shot hit this huge target – but every miss landed somewhere in the city. The French capital was not really in danger, but it was being bombarded and the Parisians panicked, believing that the Germans were much closer than they were.

This gun is sometimes erroneously called 'Big Bertha'. Big Bertha was, however, the 420-millimetre howitzer built to bombard the forts around Liège in 1914. The 210-millimetre gun that shelled Paris had no special name. On Good Friday, 29 March, 75 were killed outright, 90 were injured and many more died later, when the Church of Saint-Gervais was struck during Mass. In total, 256 Parisians were killed by the supergun. This masterpiece of German technical engineering did not affect the course of the war, but it certainly helped to harden the peace terms.

'State-sponsored Terrorism' is a phrase much used since 11 September 2001. Millions of people who would never dream of stepping in to an art gallery know Picasso's *Guernica* and recognise it as a terrifying depiction of the horrors of a calculated act of destruction on an innocent civilian population. Having learned its trade supporting the Fascists in Spain, the Luftwaffe was ready to demoralise any civilian population by flattening and burning any city centre and this became an integral part of the new style of war – *blitzkrieg.*

Hitler was delighted with the *Stuka* divebombers and warmly praised a propaganda film made by Goebbels which showed them pounding a town to rubble. The film was sent to neutral countries in the autumn of 1939 as news of the bombing of Warsaw reached Britain and France. The message was clear – make peace or the *Stukas* will get you! Rotterdam, where the entire city centre was flattened, 800–1,000 were killed and 80,000 rendered homeless, demonstrated that the Nazis were in earnest!

After Dunkirk and the fall of France there was a long pause while Hitler waited for Britain to negotiate a peace, leaving him master of Europe. Eventually it became clear that 'Operation Sealion' – the invasion of Britain – would be necessary and the Luftwaffe began the necessary 'softening-up'. At first airfields and factories – legitimate military targets – were attacked but on 23 August 1940 a few Luftwaffe aircraft missed their RAF targets and dropped their bombs on London. The British retaliated by sending a few bombers to Berlin, though little damage was caused. Three nights later the RAF were back, and this time ten people were killed. Hitler was furious. He was due to make a speech to an audience of women social workers, but deviated from his prepared script to say – 'They increase the attacks on our cities. We will raze their cities to the ground'. He ordered Goering to launch attacks on British towns – the beginning of the Blitz.

Hitler's response had been yet another use of the tactic of self-righteous indignation he had perfected in the '20s and '30s and which has been used by so many ideologues since his time. There is a troubled situation – as in the newly-formed Czechoslovakia with a sizeable minority of Sudeten Germans. There is some nationalist activity, sponsored from out-side, and some *agent provocateur* activity. The authorities clamp down and a howl of frantic outrage goes up, backed by threats of punishment. To protect the 'persecuted' the outraged party moves in and takes over.

The Blitz – myth and reality – is well-enough known to us, but by 1943 was mainly a memory. The Royal Air Force had defeated the Luftwaffe and the allies had command of the skies. At last the war was beginning to go well and most British people were now looking ahead with some confidence. However Germany had, quite literally, a secret weapon up its sleeve and its deployment from June 1944 had an important psychological effect. Yet I am not aware of any significant emphasis having been put on the v-weapons in considering the background to the bombing of Dresden. Nevertheless, I am sure that they were very much in the forefront of the minds of the British and American planners in the winter of 1944–45.

'Ihr Racker, wollt ihr ewig leben' ('Rascals, would you live for ever?' – sometimes translated as 'Dogs, would you live for ever?') is supposed to have been said, or rather, bellowed, by Frederick the Great as his Guards showed an understandable reluctance to advance at Kolin on 18 June 1757. The register he used would only have been appropriate in addressing children or animals and would have been grossly insulting to grown men. As a Great Man, Frederick was saying that he and his wishes were all that mattered and that his subjects had no value as individuals, only when organised in some way into a mass. They may have felt like pawns in some continental chess game, but in real life the pawns go back in their box after the game, ready to be set out on the board for the next time. Frederick's soldiers, their families, their enemies and the civilian populations of Central Europe, murdered, raped and looted, had no nice box to go back to.

Total disregard for the lives of subjects and contemptuous disregard for their humanity was not confined to the 18th century, nor to Prussian monarchs. It may be that they are a necessity for successful leadership, successful, that is, in the leader's terms. Certainly there are abundant examples of leaders like General Sir Redvers Buller VC, who was considerate of his men and correspondingly beloved by them – but whose indecisiveness resulted in disasters costing many unnecessary lives, lives which a more hardhearted commander would never even have put at risk. Montgomery was so appalled by his experience in the First World War that a central factor in his battle planning became the cautious minimisation of casualties – for which the gung-ho Americans criticised him. He worked hard at what he called 'bingeing up the troops' – building belief in a common enterprise for all. Yet, when the situation demanded it, he could be as logical and ruthless as any other great commander.

While even the German generals knew that defeat was inevitable once the Allies had broken out of Normandy, Hitler persisted in his belief that, as the death of the Russian Tsarina had saved Frederick the Great in the Seven Years War, every inch of territory should be held until a crop of new weapons would turn his fortunes around.

The FZG76 (German title), V-1 (official British title), or 'doodlebug' (affectionate contempt) was essentially an unmanned jet aircraft carrying a tonne of high explosive. It could be sent off in the direction of London. When the fuel ran out it fell to the ground and exploded. The V-1 was slow and flew low, so that it could be intercepted. Of the 12,000 V-1s launched against southern England only about 3,500 reached their target. At an average of one death per rocket the menace was certainly small compared with the Blitz. Nevertheless, the nervous strain was severe. Londoners thought that death from the air was a thing of the past, yet here it was again in an inhuman and capricious form, which was for some more gruelling than the Blitz had been. They had survived the Blitz, the evacuees had been brought back from the country, our boys were driving the enemy out of France, and yet this new torment was being inflicted on them.

More dangerous was the V-2, a ballistic rocket which could carry a warhead of one tonne over 225 miles. Since it flew 50 miles into the air before falling vertically on to the target it could not be defended against and gave only a few seconds notice of its imminent arrival. One thousand one hundred V-2s were fired at Britain and hundreds more were used militarily against the Allied forces after D-Day, although more people – slave workers – died building the V-2 rockets than were killed by it as a weapon.

'Die Vergeltung kommt!' (Revenge is coming!) was the Nazi propaganda slogan for the V-weapons. Much was expected of them, but their delivery was a long time coming. Development began in 1942 but for a long period there was a duel as the RAF destroyed the launching sites in the Pas de Calais and along the Dutch coast as fast as they were built. Eventually, on 12/13 June 1944, ten V-1s were dispatched. All that reached London was one lone bomb. In the second half of June, 2,000 were launched, half of which reached London. On 8 September the first V-2 rockets, despatched from The Hague, began reaching London.

Muriel Spark, semi-autobiographically or from vicarious experience, described well the capricious nature of the V-2:

From nearly a mile away comes the muffled thud of a bomb. This is one of the v-2s, for which there can be no warning siren, silently approaching and suddenly landing to demolish.

'Another one of those,' says the naval officer.

Poppy says, 'In a way I prefer no warning. You don't have to scuttle to the cellar.'

'If it's a direct hit,' says Tylden, 'nothing can save you.'

As he speaks a second explosion gives out from a distant part of London.

'Tilbury end, I think,' says Miles Bunting.

A v-2 bomb hits them direct just as the train starts pulling out. The back section of the train, where they are sitting, and all its occupants, are completely demolished.

In military terms the v-weapons were of doubtful value. When used against Antwerp almost 6,000 fell within eight miles of the city centre but only 303 fell within the boundaries of the port – which was the target. Only one ship was sunk and one dry dock was put out of action for three weeks. 3,470 Belgian civilians were killed, as compared with 682 Allied servicemen. Nevertheless, the effect of the v-weapons was to provide a major distraction to the Allied armies, whose major objective should have been the total defeat of the German forces in the field. Instead, there was pressure to divert planes and troops to the North Sea coast where the launch sites could be mopped up.

Much was expected of the electroboat, which might have revolutionised submarine development and thus reactivated the submarine war which had almost brought Britain to its knees. It came on stream too late (well after the bombing of Dresden) and therefore had no real effect on hostilities.

So what actually happened on the night of 13 February, 1945? Dresden was attacked by 1,450 British bombers. The following morning, which by grim coincidence was Ash Wednesday, 500 aircraft of the US Air Force followed in their path and also attacked several lesser targets by daylight. Why did the Allies carry out this act, which has since been characterised – not least by Goebbels two days after the event, cleverly manipulating the neutral countries – as insane barbarism?

A main element of our military policy was the mass bombing of strategic targets – factories, railways and the like – by the RAF at night and by American Flying Fortresses by day. I clearly recall when I was a youngster how the first news broadcasts of the day would report that, overnight, so many RAF bombers had attacked the marshalling yards at Hamm, or the Messerschmidt factory in Stuttgart, always concluding with the same sentence – so many 'of our planes are missing'. That meant that eight or ten times 'so many' had died a terrible death, although some might have been able to bale out only to drown in the North Sea or might now be prisoners. The highest casualty rate on a single raid was on the night of 30 March 1945, six weeks after Dresden, when Nuremberg was attacked and 96 bomber crews were lost. No doubt many of those who bombed Dresden 'bought it' that night. Does anybody feel better as a result? Nuremberg was the centre of the Nazi mass rallies and lost a fine historical core, yet no humanitarian outcry resulted.

Precision bombing had been brought to an extraordinary level by the RAF with its light Mosquito bomber. Speed, surprise, sheer technical brilliance and heroism ensured the destruction of heavy water plants and the pinpoint accuracy by means of which a Gestapo headquarters could be 'taken out', enabling the prisoners to make their escape without touching the neighbouring houses. Yet these special operations were dangerous and costly. *The Dambusters* was a gripping film with a splendid march by Eric Coates, dramatising British inventive ingenuity and operational daring, yet the operation was enormously expensive in terms of men and material and it is questionable whether it shortened the war by as much as one day.

Even in bombing raids the economies of the industrial society and of scale operated. The cheapest raid – in terms of men and material – was when a big bomber fleet, well protected by a fighter escort, flew to one big target and dropped their bomb loads in a compact pattern. Over the years Bomber Command had grown into a huge enterprise delivering vast quantities of high explosive and incendiary bombs wherever there seemed to be a large enough target.

There is a kind of military mind which struggles for 'one last push'. Napoleon's defeat at Waterloo began when he used up men, materials and time in repeated unsuccessful attacks on the fortified manor house of Hougoumont. Like Verdun in the First World War it became a prize out of all proportion to its real value and the struggle for it unbalanced everything else that followed on that day. We had these great bombing fleets at work towards the end of the war. They could only do one thing. How could we have turned off the tap? Or diverted it elsewhere?

On the other hand, after the First World War, Sir William Weir, the Air Minister, said: 'bombing has the immediate effect of causing the German to dig like the devil... this means a vast expenditure of man power'. In other words, the bombing programme was justified, not because of the simple trade-off between enemy and friendly losses, but because it tied up forces which might otherwise have been used in the front line. As long as the bombing raids continued it was necessary for the Germans to use a large proportion of Gross Domestic Product for anti-aircraft guns and fighter planes, and for reconstruction and repairs – although by 1945 much of this work was done by forced and slave labour. Although, even with this, there was a cost. Think of the manpower necessary to run the death and labour camps and the problems of moving vast numbers to them by means of a dislocated rail system. The stupidity of persisting with a bombing policy no longer necessary was matched by the stupidity – not to mention the immorality – of Hitler's Final Solution.

What was surprising was the faith still held in the demoralising effects of carpet bombing on the civilian population. The War Cabinet, 'Bomber' Harris and his circle, had lived through the London Blitz and had seen how it had failed to bring the country to its knees. Did they arrogantly assume that the German people would be less heroic and adaptable than the chirpy Cockneys as their cities were razed to the ground? There could be no defence that 'we didna ken'. The fire-storm that wiped out Hamburg in July 1943 was probably worse than the Dresden catastrophe – and the Allies knew about the results from aerial photographs and the like. Churchill, brilliantly inconsistent as ever, had broken down when viewing film of the Ruhr in 1943, asking; 'Are we beasts that we do such things? Are we taking this too far?'

Why was it considered necessary to mount these all-out raids so late in the war, when it could be said – with our 20/20 vision of hindsight – that victory was only a matter of time? But, especially in February 1945, the end was not so self-evident as we might imagine. Until Antwerp could be cleared, the Allies' communications trail was cumbersome and lengthy, while their loss of territory meant the Germans were operating with interior lines.

After six months of retreat and disaster, the Germans were now defending their homeland resolutely. The scrapings of the nation, the Hitler Youth and the aged *Volkssturm* were as loyal as the defeated *Wehrmacht*. In the Ardennes, the Americans had just been given a bloody nose. Ten weeks after the Dresden bombing, Berlin was taken by the Russians – but at a cost of 79,000 killed and over 250,000 wounded (125,000 Berliners perished in the street fighting).

By the rules of 1945, Dresden was a legitimate target because it was a centre of war production and a major communications centre. If it was legitimate to bomb the Harland and Wolff shipyard in Belfast it was surely legitimate to target munitions plants in Germany. Dresden was no longer the peaceful city of culture it had been. The Meissen porcelain factory had gone over from fragile shepherdesses to producing military teletypers – not offensive weapons but certainly crucial to the running of the *Wehrmacht*. At Zeiss-Ikon a skilled workforce – using prisoner and slave labour – of almost 14,000 was turning out bomb sights, fuses and radios.

In Dresden itself the airport we use today was built from the factory where the *Duesenberg* unmanned jet fighter was being developed at the time of the bombing. Another of the 'secret weapons', this had the potential to overturn the Allied mastery of the air in the last months of the war and so prolong the conflict till a miracle came along.

Much of Dresden's importance derives from its being a major crossroads. Here major routes from Prague and the south to Berlin, Hamburg and the north intersect west – east routes from the Rheinland and the cities of Thuringia, Leipzig and Chemnitz (soon to be renamed Karl-Marx-Stadt and since renamed yet again!) to Silesia and Poland. With hindsight it may seem curious that Chester Wilmot, in his monumental *The Struggle for Europe* barely mentions Dresden, and then only in passing as a strategic location. Presumably, in 1952, when it was published, the events at Dresden were perceived as totally marginal to the main course of the war. Throughout the war Dresden would have been a busy junction but by early 1945 the Russians were pressing very close to the east and the city had gained a great amount of additional traffic, both civil and military.

The actual impetus for the attack is explained in *Berlin: The Downfall, 1945* (Viking, London, 2002), where Antony Beevor states that:

It was intended as a rapid fulfilment of the promise to the *Stavka* to hinder German troop movements by smashing rail communications. The fact that there were 180 v-bomb attacks on England that week, the highest number so far, did little to soften the planners' hearts.

(The *Stavka* was the Soviet supreme headquarters of the armed forces, directly under Stalin's control.)

The tragedy was that, instead of troops passing through Dresden to the front, as Soviet military intelligence had asserted, the traffic was civilian and going in the opposite direction.

Knowing what we now know about Soviet tactics towards the end of the war, one wonders whether the misinformation was deliberately planted to discredit the Western Allies. There is a famous memo from Churchill on display in the Cabinet War Rooms, expressing doubts about the wisdom of bombing Dresden. Unfortunately, that is as far as it went and the raid went ahead. No doubt the good military reasons prevailed, there was the V-bomb clamour to silence and – as they say – you can't make an omelette without breaking eggs. Six weeks after the bombing Churchill cunningly repositioned himself by slipping in a little doubt about Bomber Command and its effectiveness.

Certainly, as well as Goebbels accusing us ('Anglo-American air gangsters') of war crimes and falsifying the facts, by 1950 the East Germans and Soviets saw the bombing of Dresden as a Wall Street conspiracy. 'Demos' against the bombing of Dresden were almost the only ones permitted under that regime. There may even have been a touch of racism in the virtuous concern about Dresden while, for example, choosing to forget that the: 'Americans... subjected Japan's cities to the vast fire-bombing raids which began in March 1945,' (ie just after Dresden) 'killing half a million people'. For example, more people – 100,000 – died in the 9 March Tokyo incendiary attack than were to die at Hiroshima as a result of the atomic bomb.

The problem with Dresden has been that of an over-anxious conscience. We have become used to the notion that we were the good guys in the Second World War while the enemy were Jew-killers and cathedral-bombers. While war was held to be necessary by most of society we liked to think that we fought a clean fight in the cause of right. But in the case of Dresden – despite dozens of similar bombing raids – it was felt we had gone over the score. Top Sergeant Harold W Hall, radio operator in a B-17 Flying Fortress of 527th Squadron, 379th Bomber Group, hit the nail squarely on the head when he said: 'I have to say that I felt ashamed we had levelled ourselves to the Krauts' (quoted in Taylor's *Dresden*).

My own view is that Dresden was a mistake: a particularly nasty mistake, but a mistake nevertheless. The Allies allowed themselves to be stampeded into an unnecessary over-reaction to an admittedly gloomy situation. The campaign in the West was in stagnation as the cream of the invading force had been wiped out and Hitler's makeshift armies of remnants fought to the last man. Yet the Russians were rampaging through eastern Germany. There was an understandable fury at the random terrorism of the v-bomb campaign. 'Revenge is coming!', the enemy had said. The Allies would hardly have been human had they not sought their own revenge for German atrocities. There was the leaked knowledge of the 'secret weapons' and fear of their possible impact on what was expected to be the end-game. And, as I have said, the men and material were available to deliver one final blow.

Letting Hell loose on Dresden did not shorten the war one whit. The whole gigantic operation was a wasteful blunt instrument creating waste. Waste of a fine city, waste of its population – although some of those destroyed were forced workers, supposed to be liberated by the experience. (Yet slave workers outside the city cheered the bombers, although they knew their fellows were bound to be suffering.) Waste of roads, railways and livelihoods was almost total.

For the victors, the top brass were sensitive to public opinion and tried to disentangle themselves from the consequences of their policies. Very shabby treatment was the reward for those who carried out the raid and whose only crime had been to carry out as effectively as they could the orders from those at the top. 'Bomber Harris' was the only top rank officer of World War II not to receive a major award or decoration. 125,000 flew sorties for Bomber Command. 55,573 aircrew were killed. 8,403 lucky ones were wounded and survived – although often horribly damaged. Plastic surgery and burns treatment made a great leap forward with so many guinea pigs to practise on. Another 9,838 were taken prisoner.

Of those who flew, 44.4 per cent died – a butcher's bill heavier by far than for any land battle of the Second World War and matched only by the loss incurred when a great warship was sunk 'with all hands'. The Victoria Cross is the supreme award for bravery by members of the British Armed Forces. It is an inconspicuous and simple piece of recycled bronze cannon with a purple ribbon and the briefest of citations – 'For Valour'. Nineteen Victoria Crosses were earned by Bomber Command personnel who readily went far beyond the call of duty. The bomber crews were made up of heroes, dodgers, cowards, men who were – literally – scared out of their wits and those who just plodded on and did their duty. Yet only in August 2006 was a monument unveiled in Lincoln to the men and women of Bomber Command who died in the furtherance of the national strategic bombing policy. A national disgrace.

On the day the paragraph above was written, a monument was unveiled in Westminster Abbey commemorating all those in the British services who gave their lives in the period after 1945 till the present day.

There was still no similar recognition anywhere in the national and Commonwealth capital of those who served and died in Bomber Command until, in May 2010, it was announced that Westminster City Council had given planning permission for a memorial in Green Park: 'to honour those who sacrificed everything so that we may be free today.' £2 million needed to be raised by the end of 2010 so that building could start in 2011. From January 2011 monuments ceased to be exempt from VAT, meaning that £250,000 plus £500,000 maintenance costs would be added to the bill – by now £5 million. Many are concerned that many veterans will not be around when the memorial is finished.

As Robin Gibb, President of the Heritage Foundation has said:

> This is the last truly great memorial of the two World Wars that needs to be built – and it needs to be built before it is too late. We owe the courageous men a debt of gratitude, for without them we would not be enjoying the freedom that we have today.

Fine words. Let us hope there are enough veterans left to make up a colour party on the day the memorial is unveiled.

CHAPTER 14

La Retirada – 60 years on at Argelès

ARGELÈS-SUR-MER IS NOT actually on the sea – the Mediterranean – but its suburb – Argelès-Plage – is. In the extreme south-west corner of mainland France, the Pyrenees close off miles and miles of lagoons and sandy beaches, which run, almost without interruption, from the mouth of the Rhône to the Pyrenees. Like most Mediterranean towns, Argelès is set back from the sea on a little hill, and was walled against attack from seaborne marauders of many nations. Until the Second World War this coast was swampy, the haunt of the mosquito and infested with malaria. Only a few hardy souls lived on the low ground and the *plage* consisted of a few seasonally occupied small villas and fishermen's huts.

After the war the marshes were drained, the mosquito hunted to extinction and tourist developments systematically planned into place. Elsewhere along the coast are giant tourist complexes but now Argelès is a centre for mild hedonism. Smart French ladies walk their poodles along the promenade. Elderly gents cycle back to their apartments, each with his *baguette*. Families with parasols pack the beach, which is renovated twice weekly to assure a high state of hygiene.

In and above the water at 23 degrees Celsius are swimmers, wind surfers, *parapentistes*, people rowing, paddling, sailing, diving, fishing, preparing to relax after dark at the funfair and the casino. Altogether, the Argelès area is that area in the whole of Europe with the highest concentration of campsites, apartments and hotels. Clearly this was not always true and in September 1999 the people of Argelès looked back 60 years to a turbulent and sordid incident in their past.

In Britain we have been protected from the worst excesses of 'man's inhumanity to man' by being an island, by being essentially a frivolous people who cannot concentrate on serious concerns, and by being unable to decide whether we are part of Europe or part of the United States. The details and sheer scale of foreign issues are difficult for us to grasp. Much of our knowledge and understanding of the past comes from the reading of fiction.

For Argelès George Orwell gives us a good start with the Spanish Civil War:

> The broad truth about the war is simple enough. The Spanish *bourgeoisie* saw their chance of crushing the labour movement, and took it, aided by the Nazis and by the forces of reaction all over the world.

My own understanding began on a glorious summer day just after the war, when the Granton-Burntisland ferry was reinstated for a few years, and I was able to cross to Fife with my bike and find a nice south-facing field. There I was able to read all day – and to sleep, because I found it difficult to sort out all the initials. Who were the POUM, the PSUC, the UGT? Why were the CNT and the FAI sometimes separate and sometimes hyphenated together? Why were the CEDA to be feared? I knew of the USSR, the CP and the ILP (after all, my mother was an ILP member and every week I was sent down to the paper shop for the *New Leader*) but what were the characteristics of such groups and why did they seem to be more enthusiastic about fighting each other than the enemy? Orwell describes this internal feuding very well, and the disillusion of impending defeat. Also germane to this subject is his account of leaving Catalonia and finding just over the border at Banyuls (15 kilometres from Argelès) marked coolness and lowering glances from the French.

We saw, in the context of Hellerau, how Upton Sinclair's mighty *World's End* series of novels inflamed my young mind. At a later stage Sinclair assigns to his hero, Lanny Budd, American-born but resident on the Côte d'Azur, an Italian brother-in-law who is a fighter pilot. He also has a lame duck English friend who is a left-wing activist. This gives Sinclair the opportunity to comment on the Fascist intervention in Spain. Lanny Budd has adventures of the Scarlet Pimpernel kind as he uses his own upper-class methods to help such as Alfy Pomeroy-Neilson to escape before his own unheroic retirement from the battle of Barcelona with 12 bullet holes through a Goya but none through himself.

Two recent adaptations for television of modern classic novels have been some help in building up a picture. Unfortunately, British television's love of the sumptuous recreation of period detail often results in admiration of the very attitudes the original authors were trying to satirise or denounce. In *Love in a Cold Climate* (1949), Nancy Mitford sent one of her heroines to a refugee camp near Perpignan where she laboured rather ineffectually alongside others who were more practical and more genuinely committed. But the pines on the screen were too regimented and had not been blasted by the fierce northerlies of winter. The refugees were too well fed and were dressed in outfits which, although properly researched, smelt of the couture house rather than of the march and the camp.

Evelyn Waugh is a great writer whose elegance is such that his obnoxious attitudes can be forgotten while we admire his wit. As Captain Waugh he served as Brigade Intelligence Officer to Layforce in the disastrous battle for Crete in May 1941. His experiences found their way into *Officers and Gentlemen* (1955). There he describes in a very patronising way meeting a troop of Spanish Republicans, forgetting, perhaps, that the worst that could have happened to him if he surrendered to the Germans would have been imprisonment in Colditz, but for the Catalans capture would have meant being shot out of hand. But with the collapse of the organisation of the Commonwealth force, foraging became necessary:

> ... a skill at which the Spanish Republicans proved themselves the most experienced. Waugh's Catholic prejudices evaporated when they invited him and Major General Laycock to a meal of roast sucking pig and rice.
>
> (from Antony Beevor, *Crete: The Battle and the Resistance*, Penguin, Harmondsworth, 1992)

Soldiers of Salamis (2003) by Javier Cercas has more of the smell of authenticity to it. Set in the summer of 1994, it is a 'true tale' – in effect a quest for one Miralles who:

> At the beginning of 1939 crossed the French border together with the other 450,000 Spaniards who did so in the final days of the war. On the other side was the Argelès concentration camp, which was really just a bare, immense beach surrounded by a double ring of barbed wire; there were no huts, and no protection from the savage February cold, and no sanitation, just a quagmire, where in subhuman conditions, with women and old folks and children sleeping on the sand dappled with snow and frost, and men wandering around, dumbfounded by the burden of desperation and the rancour of defeat, 80,000 Spanish fugitives waited for the hell to end.
>
> 'They called them concentration camps,' Miralles used to say. 'But they were nothing but death-traps.'
>
> And so, a few weeks after arriving in Argelès, when the enlistment flags of the French Foreign Legion appeared in the camp, Miralles signed up without a second thought.

He was in Tunisia or Algeria when war broke out and when the Vichy government was set up he followed General Leclerc across the Sahara to Chad, where they joined the Free French forces. Miralles took part in an attack on an Italian oasis in Libya – the first time a French contingent took part in an act of war against the Axis powers. After operations in French Equatorial Africa, Leclerc took his 3,200 'volunteers' across thousands of kilometres of merciless desert – on foot – to join Montgomery's Eighth Army. The division was then sent to England to train as an armoured division. After D-day they were the only French division to fight on French soil and were allowed to be the unit that liberated Paris. Miralles and his comrades from the Civil War had been fighting almost non-stop for more than seven years but now they pressed on into Germany, to get as far as Austria, where Miralles' military adventure ended. He (or the man next to him) stepped on a mine.

> He was blown to shreds. They... put him back together again as best they could. Incredibly, he survived. And slightly over a year later, there's Miralles converted into a French citizen and with a pension for life. Near Dijon.

To what extent can a 'true tale' be believed? In the centre of Nimes there is a plaque – with map – commemorating the liberation of the city on 29 August 1944 by 'elements of the First Free French Division' who covered 90,000km and lost 4,000 men – 'dead on the field of honour'. The map shows their 'battle honours' – Tunisia, Bir Hakeim, Eritrea, El Alamein, Syria, Italy, Provence, Alsace, Austria – and London! No doubt their conquests in London were of a different kind, not least because their uniforms were more stylish than our khaki serge.

The Spanish Civil War lasted from 1936 until 1939. In about 1,000 days 600,000 were killed. By February 1939 the forces of the Republican Spanish government had been comprehensively defeated by Franco's Nationalists, assisted by fellow-Fascists from Germany, Italy and Portugal. Britain was more afraid of left-wing rule than concerned for democratic government and followed a policy of non-intervention. This deprived the Republicans of support from abroad but did nothing to prevent the Kondor Legion from practising for the conquest of Europe at Guernica and elsewhere.

When resistance finally collapsed in Catalonia, rather than face the inevitable massacres which had already been a feature of Fascist victories, 500,000 Republicans fled over the snow-clad Pyrenees into a southern France which was totally unprepared for them and not at all sure that it wanted them. For example, Prats-de-Mollo, a small hillfoot town of 1,100, had to cope with 17,000. Known as *La Retirada*, this manoeuvre was seen by the Republicans as a tactical withdrawal following the last meeting of the parliament in Figueras on 1 February 1939.

Families were separated. Women and children were forced on to trains and scattered to all parts of France. The men were treated as enemies of France, disarmed and surrounded by barbed wire on the beaches of Argelès, frozen at this time of year. There they had to dig burrows in the sand like animals. Nothing had been considered regarding water supply, sanitation or shelter. Of Le Vernet, a similar camp in the Pyrenees, Arthur Koestler wrote:

> In Liberal-Centigrade, Vernet was the zero-point of infamy, measured
> in Dachau-Fahrenheit it was still thirty-two degrees above zero.

The camps in the Pyrenees were soon abandoned as the inmates froze to death in the open.

After many deaths from disease and starvation, huts, water and sanitation were provided for about 250,000 and a French hospital ship was moored offshore. Some local people protested violently at the refugees being allowed to work when they should have been sent back to Spain to be shot.

A consequence for Spain of the *Retirada* was the loss of many of high intellectual calibre – who tended to be Republicans. At Argelès the owner of the nearby Chateau de Valmy gave his house to be used as a cultural centre for the refugee writers and artists, who produced a camp newspaper which helped maintain morale. At Ceret, a hill-town nearby, many artists scraped a miserable living, often trading pictures for food and drink at the local bars. Now Ceret has a superb Museum of Modern Art where these works have been swept up for next to nothing and housed in a fine modern gallery. Prades became the home of Pablo Casals, the great cellist, who was able to use it as a base for his peaceful shaming of Franco's Spain.

Eventually the problem of how to dispose of the refugees solved itself. The entry of France and Britain into war against Germany in September 1939 meant that those who had fought against Fascism in Spain were now acceptable. Thirty-two thousand (1,900 of them British) had served in the International Brigades and could go back to their countries. Seventy thousand others at Argelès were allowed to volunteer to join the French Foreign Legion – and did so, despite the inhospitality of their treatment. Many of them served with great distinction in defending France against the Nazis, with the Resistance and with the Free French forces in Africa. Others were drafted into labour battalions to improve fortifications, were used to replace French workmen who were called up, found work locally or were just absorbed into the maelstrom of 1939–45.

However, it was not only the Republican Spaniards who fared badly at the hands of the reluctant hosts of Roussillon. Fellow French were almost as badly treated. Thirteen thousand three hundred refugees from Menton, on the Italian border, took six days in cattle trucks to get via Nice and Cannes to the Pyrenees-Orientales, although an evacuation plan had been devised to the last detail in 1938. With 30 kilos of baggage each, children, old people, the sick, the physically and mentally handicapped were dumped in 83 communes in a department with no way of housing them or giving them work.

Curiously, as the war progressed, a reverse traffic of escapees across the Pyrenees developed, with 1,000 French military police and 100 Nazi agents trying to stop them. These refugees were of four kinds. Allied personnel, particularly airmen who had been shot down, were helped by such as Donald Caskie, 'The Tartan Pimpernel'. *Evadé(e)s* who had escaped from prison or internment in France, *Réfractaires* who had fallen foul of the Vichy or German authorities, and Jews were all unacceptable in Vichy France. Once across the border there were about 800 Spanish border guards and police to avoid, with 50,000 troops within 30km of the frontier. About 55,000 civilians successfully ran this gauntlet and 700 airmen, British, American and Canadian, were 'recycled', able to fight again.

Rather pathetically, about 15,000 of the Republicans attempted the *Reconquista de Espana* on 19 October 1944. With minimal support from the French Resistance and our Special Operations people the invaders had to withdraw within the week. There were vicious reprisals in those villages in the Pyrenees where the Republicans had expected support from the Allies.

As the refugee camps at Argelès emptied they became available for another use. After the German conquest of France in 1940, only the north came under direct German control. In the south a puppet Vichy government tried to keep some national self-respect. Five days after assuming power Vichy began to legislate against 'undesirables', then foreign Jews, then French Jews. Now the camps became the destination for the undesirables of southern France (and even for some from Baden in Germany). Left-wingers, patriots and, above all, Jews, were rounded up, sent to Argelès, sorted out and packed off to slave labour in Germany and France or to Dachau and Auschwitz.

Not all the children were as fortunate as those in Montegut, where, early in 1941, 100 Jewish children were hidden in a chateau by the Swiss Red Cross. Several dozen of the new village residents under 12 were allowed to attend the school. When the children turned 18, making them subject to arrest by the Vichy authorities, local farmers took them in as labourers.

However, all semblance of normality ended at 4am on 26 August 1942. Fifty French gendarmes forced themselves into Chateau de la Hille, despite the objections of the Swiss Red Cross nurse in charge, 30-year old Rösli Näf. Thirty-nine of the older children were taken out and marched onto buses, while several dozen Montegut residents watched, many with tears in their eyes. The police commander refused to say where the children were being taken.

Näf enlisted the help of a sympathetic government bureaucrat and eventually located the children at the notorious camp at Le Vernet, 30 kilometers away. She arrived at the camp in a taxi and so surprised officials by marching in and demanding that the children be released that they let her remain in a small hut. After five days of cajoling by Näf and a Swiss Red Cross colleague in Vichy, the French relented and the children were left standing at a rail siding as hundreds of other Jewish inmates of Le Vernet were loaded on to freight wagons destined for Auschwitz.

The children returned to the chateau and went into more serious hiding until Näf was able to manage their escape to Switzerland and Spain. Ninety of the 100 children survived the war and Näf and her Swiss colleague were later honoured as righteous Gentiles by Israel's Yad Vashem Holocaust Museum.

The selectivity of memory about these times was first demonstrated to the writer in the autumn of 1957, on the way from Ulm to Munich. He had been given a lift and approaching Munich he noticed a turn-off signposted 'Dachau'.

'Dachau, Dachau. That name rings a bell,' he said.

'I don't know why,' said my German driver.

The writer persisted – 'Perhaps I heard of it in my Geography lessons at school?'

'Yes, of course,' said the driver, eagerly clutching at the proferred straw. 'It is a town well known for the manufacture of railway locomotives.'

'That must be it,' said I, unwilling to breach the rules of hospitality!

We usually associate the Nazi death camps with south and east Germany and Poland, but one of France's best kept secrets is that they had their own extermination camp at Le Struthof in the Vosges, where the unwanted would disappear *'bei Nacht und Nebel'* – under cover of night and fog. Although only about 10,000 died here, Le Struthof had its gas chambers and its gallows for public hangings. The contrast today between the calm mountain scenery and the apparatus of torture, extermination and the processing of the dead guarantees a few sleepless nights. Among the 1,120 names in the cemetery are those of two British women. When I visited the camp and saw these names I constructed my own horror story – involving nice tweed-clad girls with cut-glass accents, as in the war films – to explain this simple fact.

It gave me no pleasure in 2005 to discover how near the truth I had been. Vera Leigh (41) was a dress designer and Diana Rowden (29) was a journalist. Both were based in Paris and both were Special Operations Executive agents of Churchill's Secret Army who had been flown into France to support the French Resistance. They were captured and tortured by the Nazis. On 6 July 1944 they were taken to Le Struthof and executed by lethal injection later the same day.

In 1943, the Vichy government brought in a Compulsory Labour Scheme or STO (*Service du Travail Obligatoire*), under which almost a million 'volunteers', French and stateless, were shipped off to work in Germany and on the Atlantic Wall. Again the camps were pressed into service for collection and despatch of these lost souls, most destined to die from disease, malnutrition and, ironically, the Allied bombing of such targets as the Krupp arms factories.

In many French towns the war memorial is not a simple list of names of those who died for *'La Patrie'*. With characteristic French precision it is common practice to classify the 'victims of two wars' as, for example, on the memorial at the railway workshops of Arles. There we can separate out:

Died in concentration camps
Forced labour deportees
Shot by the Germans
Victims of Bombardment (what we now call, euphemistically, 'friendly fire')

'What did you do in the War, Daddy?' is still not a question to be asked lightly in France, but the Argelès of today is to be admired for facing up to its past, even although it has taken 60 years. February 1999 would have been the time to observe the anniversary of the *Retirada* but there would have been no-one around to take part. Instead, at the end of the summer season in September there was no lack of interest. There were exhibitions, conferences, debates, and films at a number of venues around *l'Espace Liberté.* At one of the discussions at Argelès it was agreed that the camps be referred to at this late date as 'accommodation camps', rather than 'concentration camps'!

At one exhibition old ladies pointed out their younger selves in camp photos. An old man in a beret named the people on a truck loaded for Auschwitz. Saturday. 4 September, was the big day. One of the roads through Argelès which had been followed by more than 250,000 Spanish Republicans was renamed *'l'Avenue de la Retirada 1939'.*

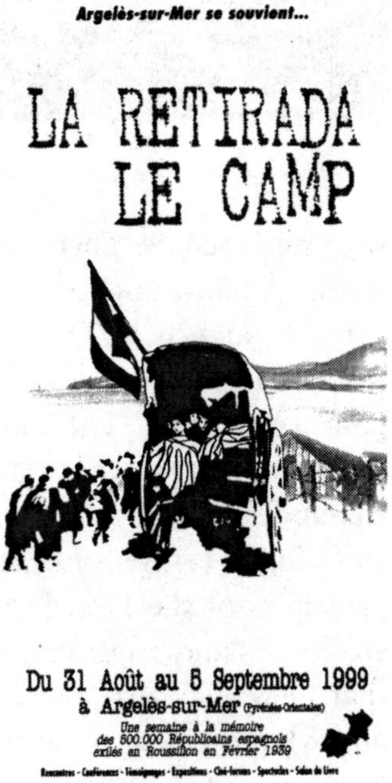
Argelès-sur-Mer se souvient...
LA RETIRADA
LE CAMP
Du 31 Août au 5 Septembre 1999
à Argelès-sur-Mer (Pyrénées-Orientales)
Une semaine à la mémoire
des 500.000 Républicains espagnols
exilés en Roussillon en Février 1939
Rencontres - Conférences - Témoignages - Expositions - Ciné-forums - Spectacles - Salon du Livre

FIG. 23
'Argelès remembers'
– 1999 programme.

Just outside the town is the cemetery for the children who died in the camp. Although there is no irrigation and the garden is very limited as a result, a commemorative oak was planted by the obelisk with the children's names. There are 69 names on the memorial, including Goldberg – the only one without an initial. The memorial was donated by one MN Goldberg of Antwerp. Is there another untold story here?

Where the main entrance to the camp had been is now the Rue des Dunes between

the Grand Hotel du Lido and a block of holiday apartments. On the Saturday a monolith with a plaque was officially inaugurated at this spot. When unveiled it bore the inscription:

> To the memory of the
> 100,000 Spanish Republicans
> interned in the camp of
> Argelès after the *RETIRADA*
> of February 1939.
>
> Their misfortune was to
> have struggled to defend
> Democracy and the
> Republic against fascism in
> Spain from 1936 to 1939.
>
> Free man, remember.
> (*Homme libre, souviens toi.*)

FIG. 24
Argelès – *La Retirada*, children's monument.

Veterans and holiday-makers crowded around. There were flags and medals. There was a fly-past with trails of red, white and blue smoke. Chic young reporters asked inane questions of old men who had been through hell. The public address system failed but an old soldier reminded us in clear Catalan why we were here and what had happened here. (PLATE 8A) The minister who had flown down especially from Paris for this Saturday afternoon apologised for the suffering of the Republicans in the land of *The Rights of Man*. He reminded us of the suffering of refugees in Europe today and called on us to rally round the principles of the French Republic – Liberty, Equality, Fraternity. There were tears and approving nods (although honesty compels me to record that there was also a scuffle between a lean, hard man with a big dog and what seemed to me to be an innocent bystander).

So we left wondering at the endurance of those old men and women who had seen so much and survived so much, lifted in spirit by their example, but uneasy at our likely reactions if we were ever so unfortunate as to face the kinds of challenge they faced.

Three Afterthoughts

1   The little ceremony described above can be construed as recognition by the French of the shabbiness of the treatment they dealt out to the Republican refugees and as a kind of belated apology.

In 1999, official records in Spain still referred to these people as 'bandits' and 'brigands'. Such references were struck off in spring 2001. The Law of Recuperation of Historical Memory of 1 November 2006 gave the few survivors the right to a military pension. See also 3) below.

2   In 2005, I was involved in a botanical exploration in the eastern Pyrenees, in Spanish Catalonia. At Ripoll, midway between Barcelona and the French border at Puigcerdà, we were assembling for the day when I was approached by a gentleman a little younger than myself who had been observing us closely since breakfast. It turned out that he was on his way from a holiday on the Costa Brava to his home near Toulouse. As a babe in arms he had been carried through four feet of snow over the Col d'Ares by his mother, his father having been shot by the fascists. His mother went to work on a French farm and eventually married the farmer, who brought up the little refugee boy as if he were his own. So far as one can tell in a quarter of an hour, the little boy is now a well-integrated and solid citizen, able to cross and recross frontiers without bitterness.

Later in the day we were at the Col, where the track was made into a tarred road after the Second World War, complete with frontier and customs posts. Now these have been demolished. France and Spain are community neighbours and there are no obstacles to the free movement of their citizens.

And so we have a happy ending. In 1999 all was harmony around the monument in Argelès. Revolutionaries and counter-revolutionaries had subordinated their passions to peaceful co-existence. In the latter part of the 20th century the prospect of history repeating itself seemed unthinkable as we settled into a comfortable, if slightly dull, existence.

Now, however, there is a change in the air. We have had the Twin Towers in New York and the Atocha Station in Madrid. The old hatreds – class, religion, colour – can be sniffed around. Like Burns in *To A Mouse: On Turning Her Up in Her Nest with the Plough, November 1785*:

I backward cast my e'e,
On prospects drear!
An' forward, tho' I canna see,
I guess and fear!

3　In the National Edition of *El Mundo* of 13 September 2008 there was a two-page spread on 'The Judicial Revision of Francoism', with photographs, detailed location maps and two diagrams illustrating the methods by which the remains of Franco's opponents are being exhumed.

For years there was a conspiracy of silence about the excesses of the Civil War and there was a Law of Amnesty in 1977. In recent years, however, it has been recognised that letting sleeping dogs lie does not help nation-building and that true reconciliation can only be achieved when all the causes of offence have been brought out into the open and the victims of oppression are given a decent burial.

FIG. 25
Mass graves in Catalonia.
(*El Mundo*, 13 September 2008)

CHAPTER 15

'For I will give you the Morning Star'

IT WAS ONE OF my mother's contributions to my upbringing, by precept and example, to have a healthy appreciation of the interest and importance of cemeteries. Yet, even before going round the cemetery, in a strange town or village it is necessary to inspect the war memorial commemorating those who gave their lives for King and country in the Great War – 'the war to end all wars' – in so many respects the turning-point of our modern history. So much can be learned about the town or parish from the recorded names, dates and regiments.

The proportion of Scots in the armed services was twice as great as for the rest of the United Kingdom and the butcher's bill was also twice as high. This is rammed home on the Scottish National War Memorial in Edinburgh Castle, which must be our finest and most touching record of those times. Appropriately on the highest point of Edinburgh Castle, an old barrack block was recycled by Robert Lorimer and dedicated in 1927 as a national shrine, a memorial and a record of the individuals killed in the Great War.

A Hall of Honour holds memorials to the regiments and other units who served, with their statistics and battle honours. Open Rolls of Honour list those who made the ultimate sacrifice. In the shrine some of the native rock on which the Castle is built symbolises the land from which those who died came. A great steel casket contains the Rolls of Honour. A very fine bronze frieze shows the combatants of all ranks and branches of the services. Overall, the effect is sombre and dignified, but not partisan. The stained glass and sculpture are beautiful if, perhaps, somewhat idealised – but what else could be expected with the scars of war so fresh? Would we want the recently bereft to know the macabre details of how their loved ones met their fate?

As a youngster, the Memorial was approached with hushed reverence which turned to bewilderment in the face of the numbers – the numbers killed in the various regiments, the number of books – the Rolls of Honour – each with so many pages and with so many names to the page.

No part of the country was unaffected, but the long lists seem most poignant in what are now the empty places. While each death must have been unique to someone, the loss of 20 young men from a Highland valley, where the community itself might be in danger of dying out, must have been an unimaginable blow.

A year or two ago I spent the time around Armistice Sunday in the Gordon Highlanders country of Aberdeenshire and Banffshire. In the years between the Boer War and the First World War my grandfather was the postie in The Cabrach. When I was young he regaled me with the characteristics of every croft and farm, and his adventures there in the fierce winters. Global warming was not even a concept in the early 20th century! Rural depopulation has emptied The Cabrach and now all that remains of the places that were good for a cup of tea, or a dram, or nothing at all, are names on an old map and a few ruined gable ends of cottages.

One contributing factor was the slaughter of the cream of the country. Driving round the Gordons' hinterland there are dozens of villages, each with its war memorial, and rural crossroads in small parishes, with lists and lists and lists of young men who left the peewits' cry of their country-side for ever.

Tarland is a large village with the war memorial in the middle of the square. Among the Second World War names are those of Lady MacRobert's three sons, who all served in the RAF. Her reaction to this family tragedy was to buy a bomber, donate it to the RAF, and have it named 'MacRobert's Reply'. In the square, Tarland's biggest shop had one of its large plate glass windows given over to an Armistice Day display, with photographs, documents and several kilts – the 'yellow thread in the Gordon plaid' – prominent.

Some memorials unconsciously display a savage irony. Thus, on Harris and Lewis the memorials give the dates of the Great War as from 1914 to 1919. This has nothing to do with the date of the Versailles peace treaty – remembering that the 11th day of the 11th month was only an Armistice, a ceasefire, and not the formal end of the war. Instead, the 1919 date refers to a terrible and avoidable loss of life among a group who had every reason to feel euphoric at having successfully got through the greatest struggle in Europe up to that date.

In 1968, Francis Thompson wrote in his *Lewis and Harris*:

Those in Harris and Lewis aged 50 or over have their recollections charged with little else than disaster. Not only did the island lose an abnormally high percentage of its young men in the 1914 war, but some 200 of those who survived the holocaust were lost in the wreck of the *Iolaire* on New Year's morning, 1919 – the first morning of the first new year of peace, literally within sight of home.

The *Iolaire* was bringing soldiers and sailors back from the war to their homes when she ran on to some rocks just outside Stornoway. She was expected and there was therefore a good turnout of wives and children waiting to welcome their loved ones home. Instead they had the doubtful pleasure of watching their sons and fathers drowning little more than a stone's-throw from the shore. No community on the islands was spared as over 200 of the male population were wiped out in a matter of minutes.

The jury at the Court of Inquiry found:

> that the *Iolaire* went ashore and was wrecked on the rocks inside the 'Beasts of Holm' (outside Stornoway) about 1.55 on the morning of 1 January, resulting in the death of 205 men; that the officers in charge did not exercise sufficient prudence in approaching the harbour; that the boat did not slow down, and that the look-out was not on duty at the time of the accident; that the number of lifeboats, boats and rafts was insufficient for the number of people carried, and that no orders were given by the officers with a view to saving life; and, further, that there was a loss of valuable time between the signals of distress and the arrival of life-saving apparatus in the vicinity of the wreck.

Rosebank Cemetery, on the Edinburgh–Leith boundary, has one of the most poignant of memorials. The 7th Battalion of the Royal Scots was a Territorial Battalion recruited mainly in Leith. As Territorials they were not required to serve abroad, but they volunteered for foreign service and on 22 May 1915 they were on a troop train heading south from Larbert for Liverpool, where they would embark for Gallipoli. At the signal box at Quintinshill, near Gretna, there was a cosy arrangement between the signalmen about the changeover between shifts. The result was a sequence of terrible events that would appear totally improbable if they were part of a disaster movie of our time.

A local train (on which the late-arriving signalman, Tinsley, had come from Carlisle) was shunted on to the opposite line to allow a late north-bound express to make up time. It was promptly forgotten. Minutes later, thundering from the north came the troop train at 70mph, ploughing at full speed into the stationary goods train. With the usual British disregard for the poor bloody infantry, the rolling stock making up the troop train was obsolete and the wooden carriages – and the passengers – disintegrated into smithereens. The train was gas-lit, with the gas-oil in tanks under the carriages. Burning coal and escaped gas formed a lethal cocktail, the result being an inferno which took over 24 hours to extinguish and which rendered dozens of bodies unrecognisable.

As a final indignity, just as the first survivors were beginning to disentangle themselves from the wreckage, the late express came hurtling through to cause further carnage. It was four hours before the fire brigade arrived. Yet worse was to come. At the end of the day about 60 survivors, dishevelled and demoralised, were rounded up and taken south to the barracks in Carlisle, where:

> On their march from the railway to the barracks they were mistaken for
> prisoners of war and stoned by the watching crowd.

This was by far the worst railway accident in British history, although wartime censorship kept the details quiet. Two hundred and twenty-seven people died, 215 of them Royal Scots, and 246 were injured. Many of the bodies were taken back to the Dalmeny Street drill hall in Leith before a succession of funerals with full military honours trudged down to the far corner of Rosebank Cemetery. The local papers carried photographs of the cortèges coming down Pilrig Street for as far as the eye could see.

What happened to the survivors? What about post-traumatic stress syndrome? As a local catastrophe the result was even more vigorous recruiting in Leith. The 7th Royal Scots were made up to strength by drafts from other units and joined the 4th and 5th Battalions in the Dardanelles in mid-June. The terrain was hostile, artillery support was minimal and the Turks were ferocious defenders of their homeland. Typhoid, cholera and dysentery were rampant. The cost of the attack of 28 June was appalling. The 4th and 7th that day lost 337 killed and missing and almost 300 wounded. The dry scrub went on fire and many of the wounded burned to death where they lay, having gone from the frying pan of Gretna into the fire of Gallipoli.

In The Diamond, in the city then called Londonderry and now known as Derry, is a splendid war memorial with the names of the 756 individuals from the city who died during the Great War. Of these, 115 died on 1 July 1916, the notorious first day of the Battle of the Somme and the bloodiest in the history of the British army. There were 60,000 casualties, most of them in the first hour. Many others died of wounds in the following weeks. But for those mourning at home there was at least the consolation that their sons had died well, doing their duty and facing the enemy. The loyalty and fortitude of the sons of Ulster has passed into folk memory and have even been celebrated in a successful play by Frank McGuinness, *Observe the Sons of Ulster Marching towards the Somme*.

But no such consolation could be felt by the people of the Hebrides or of Leith, the lives of whose loved ones had been carelessly thrown away by the stupidity and incompetence of those responsible for their good management. In Iraq and Afghanistan today we hear of the Military Covenant, the unspoken agreement that a soldier will march and fight and even lay down his life but in return he should be well led and properly equipped. Clearly in Britain in World War 1 there was no such covenant and it was back to Frederick the Great and 'Dogs, will you live for ever?'

Most of these war memorials are fairly conventional in their design and arrangement. With so many being commissioned at the same time it is no surprise to find standard designs with long lists on the sides of a large block on whose top glowers a resolute Highlander or a sturdy infantryman with puttees and fixed bayonet.

The most outrageous monument must be at Glenelg, a huge parish on the Invernessshire mainland facing over to Skye, but with few residents. The old crofters were cleared from the wild and inhospitable interior down to the coastal strip. It is there, next to Kyle Rhea, the channel between the mainland and Skye, that one turns a corner to be knocked over by the most grandiose of sculptured groups. It would not be out of place in a French provincial town, but here, with the sea and the hills of Skye beyond, it is a display of panache in the face of sorrow.

A winged Victory, with her laurel wreath, rises from the tangle of a broken drum, a discarded knapsack, a broken crown and a tentative dove of peace. She towers over a superbly constructed maiden who reaches up to Victory's graciously extended hand. Meanwhile, a moustachioed Highlander, accoutred in kilt, balmoral and puttees, with ammunition pouches and a tin hat, modestly averts his eyes from the unseemly display of abundant female flesh. (PLATE 8B)

The roll of those who gave their lives is also unusual. Of the 16 from World War I (four from World War II) only six were from local regiments, five from the Camerons and one Seaforth. Two were from the Canadians and there was a New Zealander – presumably men who had emigrated from Glenelg before 1914 but had joined up to come back to Europe to serve the country of their birth. There were two Captains from the 7th Battalion of the Queen's Regiment (the 2nd of Foot, based in Surrey) and two from the cavalry. Major Valentine Fleming was from the Oxfordshire Yeomanry and his name and presence among the dead provide an explanation for this exotic display of grief and gratitude in such an unlikely place.

Valentine Fleming (1882–1917) was the son of Robert Fleming, a wealthy Scottish banker. The Flemings were big landowners in the parish of Glenelg. They also had an estate at Huntercombe, in Oxfordshire, which accounts for the cavalry connection. Fleming was killed on 20 May 1917, was awarded a posthumous DSO and was the subject of an appreciation in *The Times* by Winston Churchill.

Major Fleming's widow – Evelyn St Croix Rose Fleming – inherited the large estate in trust, which made her a very wealthy woman. Should she ever re-marry, the trust would cut her out, thus ensuring that she would remain forever a widow, regardless of other loves or circumstances. (She and Fleming had been married on St Valentine's Day). Her older son, Peter, acquired some celebrity as a traveller in Central Asia and served with distinction in the Second World War. One of his travel books was made a home reader in some of our more forward-looking post-war schools, but he is pretty well forgotten today.

Her younger son, Ian, grew up in the shadow of his brilliant brother and had a rather unsatisfactory career. Fairly late on, however, (he was only 56 when he died) he created the character of James Bond and – as they say – the rest is history.

With a background like hers it is not surprising that the widow was not content with the usual foursquare monument. Instead she clearly commissioned someone from the Beaux Arts tradition (although the monument carries no attribution) to let his emotions run freely. A truly splendid gesture.

By contrast, Arbuthnot, in Kincardineshire, is a small rural parish with a modest kirk and kirkyard. In it is a modest stone, now decaying, 'for the memory of James Leslie Mitchell (Lewis Grassic Gibbon)', with his dates. On the village hall, a few yards away, is a plain, simple but quite remarkable plaque. As the granite memorials of Aberdeenshire reflect the land from which those who died came – hard, dour, but enduring – and Glenelg commemorates the rich and hierarchical provider of its monument, so Arbuthnot embo-

FIG. 26
War Memorial, Parish of Arbuthnott.

dies the intimate relationship between its people and the land.

Most memorials list the dead in military fashion, by reference to the units they served in. The arrangement is usually hierarchical – senior officers at the top, down to the privates, gunners, seamen or whatever at the bottom or round the sides. Decorations are usually listed.

At Arbuthnot, however, the arrangement is quite simple – names in egalitarian alphabetical order down the left hand side and opposite each name the place, farm or croft, he originated from. The dedication is:

> In grateful memory of the men belonging to the Parish of Arbuthnott who sacrificed their lives for the good of humanity in the Great War 1914–1919.

Again, the egalitarian touch. These men would have felt like JC Milne's *The Patriot*:

> Fecht for Britain? Hoot awa!
> For Bonnie Scotland? Imph, man, na!
> For Lochnagar? Wi' clook and claw!

These men did not die for a far-off King or an amorphous Commonwealth but for a simpler, nobler, ideal. The good of humanity is above jingoism.

It can be no coincidence that Lewis Grassic Gibbon should be buried a few yards off. No writer has better expressed than he the love–hate relationship between the peasant and the land, particularly in *Sunset Song*. It begins with a wonderful survey of sequent occupance, like Mr Filmer's in my introduction, as Grassic Gibbon traces the story of the Kinraddie lands from the time of the Picts. Through the medium of a young Chris Guthrie there is brought out the struggle between the desire for material advancement and gentrification, and the primal pull of the land, the soil, and the folk memory.

The last few pages describe the unveiling of the Kinraddie memorial. The locals thought that the minister would:

> have a fine stone angel, with a night-gown on, raised up at
> Kinraddie cross-roads.[1]

Instead he:

> had the old stone circle by Blawearie loch raised up and cleaned and set
> all in place, real heathen-like.

On the day, the minister preached from the text: 'For I will give you the Morning Star', reminding the folk present of those who had gone 'from the lands they loved', that they were: 'the Last of the Peasants, the last of the Old Scots folk'. Although they had died for a world that was past they had not died for the world 'we seem to inherit'. Instead he saw: 'a greater hope and a newer world undreamt when these four died'. Then occurred a scene familiar and moving to people of my generation:

> The Highland man McIvor tuned up his pipes and began to step slow
> round the stone circle by Blawearie Loch: slow and quiet, and folk
> watched him, the dark was near, it lifted your hair and was eerie and
> uncanny, the *Flowers of the Forest* as he played it. It rose and wept and
> cried, that crying for the men that fell in battle... He fair could play, the
> piper, he tore at your heart marching there with the tune leaping up the
> moor and echoing across the loch.

As night falls, the Kinraddie folk disperse and we are left with Chris and the minister looking to a future together.

A monument must record the best about the whole messy business. Dying for the good of humanity must seem naïve to many observers. The minister, in his address, strikes a note of ambiguity which resonates better to those of us with the gift of hindsight. The only thing that does not ring true about this last scene from *Sunset Song* is that there are only four names on the Kinraddie memorial – even a little parish like Arbuthnot had 12 and most had dozens.

Throughout these Random Thoughts two currents seem to have been running. One has to do with the wonderful world we live in, its beauty, its complexity, its power to make us stop and admire. Yet, perversely, we seem to enjoy being as savage towards each other as our level of technology can contrive. Again and again one finds oneself quoting Burns:

Man's inhumanity to Man
Makes countless thousands mourn.

Such waste, not just of lives, but of finite resources. The Israelis scattered 3½ million anti-personnel mines in Lebanon subsequent to agreeing to an UN solution. At £10 a time – surely far too cheap – that could have been £35 million for reconciliation, rather than a spiteful (and painful) gesture.

In *The Bridge on the Drina,* Nobel prizewinner Ivo Andri brings the book to a close by describing the last few minutes of Alihodja's life. For centuries the bridge had stood, had been maintained and had been improved. Then one day it had been blown:

into the skies as if it had been some stone in a mountain quarry and not a thing of beauty and value, a bequest.

Perhaps, thinks the *hodja:*

If they destroy here, then somewhere else someone else is building. Surely there are still peaceful countries and men of good sense who know of God's love?

He hopes that great and wise men should not vanish from the world. 'That could not be.'

Lewis Grassic Gibbon's later books show how naïve Chris and her minister were in facing the future with confidence. The recent history of the Balkans makes one question the realism of Alihodja's last wish, that the good in Man may outgrow the evil. It may be that it is our fate to jog along as Alihodja suggests, with a bit of good being done there and a little bit of evil being done there until the day comes when – aided by technology – a little bit of evil gets out of control, the result being to, as Charles Murray ('Hamewith') wrote in *Gin I was God:*

Droon oot the hale hypothec.[2]

Note

[1] A cheap imitation of the Glenelg monument, all that a poor parish could afford.

[2] Anglicé: 'Drown out the whole caboodle.'

A Random Bibliography

RANDOM THOUGHTS COME from a kaleidoscope of stimuli, most of them untraceable. So much of one's knowledge has been absorbed by a kind of osmotic process into the conscious, the subconscious and the unconscious, that detailed references and bibliographies for each contribution are just not possible. Having said that, some readers may itch to know more, or to challenge my views or my sources. For their sakes, some important references are given below when not self-evident from the main body of text. They are arranged, not randomly, but by topic.

The Random Thoughts of a Random Fellow
Ernest Raymond, *A Chorus Ending* (Cassell, London, 1951)

The Cradle of the Sublime and The Wolf's Glen
WEK Anderson (ed.), *The Journal of Sir Walter Scott* (Canongate Books, Edinburgh, 1998)
Anna Bennett (translator), *Art Book, Friedrich* (Dorling Kindersley, London, 1999)
Alain de Botton, *The Art of Travel* (Hamish Hamilton, London, 2002)
Rose-Marie and Rainer Hagen, *Masterpieces in Detail: What Great Paintings Say* (Taschen, Cologne, 2000)
John Leighton and Colin J Bailey, *Caspar David Friedrich: Winter Landscape* (The National Gallery, London, 1990)
Simon Schama, *Landscape and Memory* (HarperCollins, London, 1995)
John Warrack, *Carl Maria von Weber* (Hamish Hamilton, London, 1968)
Pamela Weston (ed), *Fifty Classical Studies for Clarinet* (Fentone Music, Corby, 1976)

The Mind Grows Giddy
Stephen Baxter, *Revolutions in the Earth* (Weidenfeld & Nicolson, London, 2003)
GH Mitchell, EK Walton and Douglas Grant (eds), *Edinburgh Geology: An Excursion Guide* (Oliver and Boyd, Edinburgh and London, 1960)

The Grand Staircase
Chet Raymo, *The Crust of Our Earth: An Armchair Traveler's Guide to the New Geology* (Prentice-Hall, Inc, Englewood Cliffs, New Jersey, 1983)

On Hearing the First Delius of Spring

Stuart Benn, *Mountain Birds* (in *Hostile Habitats: Scotland's Mountain Environment*, Scottish Mountaineering Trust, 2006)

Gordon D'Arcy, *The Guide to the Birds of Ireland* (Irish Wildlife Publications, Dublin, 1981)

Frank Fraser Darling, *A Herd of Red Deer* (ed.Walter Stephen) (Luath Press Ltd, Edinburgh, 2008)

JTR Sharrock, *The Atlas of Breeding Birds in Britain and Ireland* (British Trust for Ornithology and Irish Wildbird Conservancy, Tring 1976)

Ian Wyllie, *The Cuckoo* (BT Batsford Ltd, London, 1981)

RLS and the God-like Sculptor

Jenni Calder, *RLS: A Life Study* (London, 1980)

John H Dryfhout, *The Work of Augustus Saint-Gaudens* (University Press of New England, Hanover, New Hampshire, 1982)

JC Furnas, *Voyage to Windward: The Life of Robert Louis Stevenson* (London, 1952)

James Pope Hennessy, *Robert Louis Stevenson* (Jonathan Cape, London, 1974)

Musée des Augustins, Toulouse, *Augustus Saint-Gaudens 1848–1907: A Master of American Sculpture* (Somogy, Paris, 1999)

Rosaline Masson, *The Life of Robert Louis Stevenson* (W & R Chambers Edinburgh, 1924)

Robert Louis Stevenson, *Letters, vol. IV; 1891–94* (London, 1926)

Peeling a Dutch Onion

J Davidson and A Gray, *The Scottish Staple at Veere* (Longmans Green, London, 1909)

William Croft Dickinson, *Scotland from the Earliest Times to 1603* (Thomas Nelson, London, 1962)

Michael Lynch (ed.), *The Early Modern Town in Scotland* (Croom Helm, London, 1987)

Michael Lynch, Michael Spearman and Geoffrey Stell (eds), *The Scottish Medieval Town* (John Donald, Edinburgh, 1988)

GE Lythe, *The Economy of Scotland in its European Setting 1550–1625* (Oliver and Boyd, Edinburgh, 1960)

Christine McGladdery, *James II* (John Donald, Edinburgh, 1997)

TC Smout, *Scottish Trade on the Eve of the Union 1660–1707* (Oliver and Boyd, Edinburgh, 1963)

Hendrik Willem van Loon, *The Home of Mankind* (Harrap, London, 1933 reprint, endpaper)

Hendrik Willem van Loon, *Van Loon's Lives* (Harrap, London, 1943)

Marvel Upon Marvel

Actes du Colloque de Nice, *La Frontière des Alpes-Maritimes de 1860 à Nos Jours* (Editions Serre, Nice, 1992)

Frédéric Touchet, *Fortifications du 16e siècle à aujourd'hui* (Le Nez en l'air, Lyon, 2003)

Hellerau – Dream turned Nightmare

Upton Sinclair, *A World to Win* (T Werner Laurie, London, 1947)

Upton Sinclair, *World's End* (T Werner Laurie, London, 1940)

Frederick Taylor, *Dresden: Tuesday 13 February 1945* (Bloomsbury, London 2004)

Reprint (1996) of: *Das Junge Hellerau* (Anon) (Hellerau-Verlag, Dresden 1996)

'Die Vergeltung kommt!'

Antony Beevor, *Berlin: The Downfall, 1945* (Viking, London, 2002)

Alistair Horne, *Seven Ages of Paris: Portrait of a City* (Pan Books, London, 2003)

Rupert Matthews, *Hitler: Military Commander* (Arcturus, London, 2003)

Martin Middlebrook, *The Kaiser's Battle: 21 March 1918, The First Day of the German Spring Offensive* (Allen Lane, London, 1978)

Muriel Spark, *The Hothouse by the East River* (Macmillan, London, 1973)

Frederick Taylor, *Dresden: Tuesday 13 February 1945* (Bloomsbury, London 2004)

Chester Wilmot, *The Struggle for Europe* (Collins, London, 1952)

La Retirada – 60 Years on at Argelès

Antony Beevor, *Crete: The Battle and the Resistance* (Penguin, Harmondsworth, 1992)

Antony Beevor, *The Spanish Civil War* (Cassell, London, 1982)

Marc Dubin, *The Rough Guide to the Pyrenees* (Rough Guides, New York, London, Delhi, 2004)

George Orwell, *Homage to Catalonia* (Penguin, Harmondsworth, 1962)

Ian Ousby, *Occupation: The Ordeal of France 1940–1944* (Pimlico, London, 1999)

Upton Sinclair, *Wide is the Gate* (T Werner Laurie, London, 1941)

'For I will give you the Morning Star'

Lewis Grassic Gibbon, *A Scots Quair* (Jarrolds, London, 1946)

The Evolution of Evolution: Darwin, Enlightenment and Scotland

Walter Stephen

ISBN 978 1906817 23 7 PBK £12.99

What led Darwin to form his theory of evolution? To what extent did the Enlightenment influence Darwin's work? How did Scots help Darwin to publish the most successful and controversial book of his time?

In 1825 Darwin began to study medicine at Edinburgh University, the seat of the Enlightenment. The Enlightenment had created a thirst for science, and in his two years at Edinburgh, Darwin became involved with the people and ideas that were to shape the world's understanding of the natural sciences, including Darwin's concept of evolution and natural selection.

The Evolution of Evolution *is a well researched and thoughtfully written book that recognises the importance of Scotland in the formation of evolutionary thinking and the role of Scots in both mentoring and influencing Charles Darwin throughout his life.*

SCOTTISH REVIEW OF BOOKS

A Herd of Red Deer

Frank Fraser Darling (edited and introduced by Walter Stephen)

ISBN 978 1906307 42 4 PBK £9.99

Frank Fraser Darling was an ecologist, a conservationist, and a prophet. He was the first naturalist to leave the laboratory and the library to spend long periods observing and recording our largest land mammal in its mountain habitat – our last great wilderness. The David Attenborough of his day, Fraser Darling inspired a generation to follow in his footsteps, and to love natural history and the Highlands.

A Herd of Red Deer is the result of two years spent in one of the most hostile environments in the British Isles, following the seasonal wanderings of the deer through the fly season, the rut, facing the winter and rearing fawns in the spring. Fraser Darling studies changes in the herds to build up a moving and emotive picture of the life of the red deer.

Think Global, Act Local: Life and Legacy of Patrick Geddes

Edited by Walter Stephen
ISBN 978 1842820 79 7 PBK £12.99

 Town planning. Interest-led, open-minded education. Preservation of buildings with historical worth. Community gardens. All are so central to modern society that our age tends to claim these notions as its own. In fact they were first visualised by Sir Patrick Geddes, a largely forgotten Victorian Scot and one of the greatest forward thinkers in history.

Gardener, biologist, conservationist, social evolutionist, peace warrior, and town planner, Geddes spent many years conserving and restoring Edinburgh's historic Royal Mile at a time when most decaying buildings were simply torn down. With renovation came educational ideas such as the development of the Outlook Tower, numerous summer schools and his Collège des Écossais in Montpellier. In India much of Geddes's belief in people planning can be seen, taking the form of pedestrian zones, student accommodation for women, and urban diversification projects.

A Vigorous Institution: The Living Legacy of Patrick Geddes

Edited by Walter Stephen
ISBN 978 1905222 88 9 PBK £12.99

 Patrick Geddes was an original thinker and innovator, an internationalist steeped in Scottishness. His achievements included conservation projects in the Old Town of Edinburgh and in London; community development through greening the urban environment; and town plans for Dunfermline, Cyprus, Tel Aviv and over 50 Indian cities. He pioneered summer schools and self-governing student hostels, used public art to stimulate social change, and established his own College of Art in Edinburgh and a Collège des Écossais in Montpellier.

Aspects of his life are re-examined in an attempt to further understand his thinking. How much of an anarchist was he? How influential were his home and childhood experiences? Why did he change his name and why – till the publication of this book – was his birthhouse shrouded in mystery?

Willie Park Junior: The Man Who Took Golf to the World

Walter Stephen

ISBN 978 1905222 21 6 HBK £25

Nineteenth century Musselburgh, Scotland, was a hotbed of golfing genius, and one of the greats was Willie Park Junior.

Twice winner of the Open, Park also played challenge and demonstration matches at home and abroad. His career in golf course design took him from Britain to Western Europe and then North America; in total Park laid out over 160 courses worldwide, many of which are still in use today.

After a century of improved golf technology – better clubs, a larger ball, and more tailored course layouts – what legacy has Willie Park Junior left to the modern golfer? Walter Stephen tours us round some of Park's best-loved courses to see how they have stood the tests of time and tee-off.

a book that is quirky, idiosyncratic, frustrating and ultimately as fascinating as the game itself.
THE HERALD

The Game of Golf

Willie Park Junior (edited and introduced by Walter Stephen)

ISBN 978 1905222 65 0 HBK £12.99

The golfer Willie Park Junior speaks out and voices his opinions on golfing equipment and techniques. Straight from the man who brought golf from Scotland to the world comes a comprehensive guide to playing golf that compliments the game of players of all skill levels.

Every aspect of playing, from selecting equipment to proper swing and grip, is explained in detail and given beside the opinion and tips of a successful 19th century golf champion. This commentary reveals the finer details of the game and original techniques that can still be applied today. Including a helpful glossary and diagrams and illustrations, the history and art of golf are revealed.

Details of these and other books published by Luath Press can be found at:
www.luath.co.uk

Luath Press Limited
committed to publishing well written books worth reading

LUATH PRESS takes its name from Robert Burns, whose little collie Luath (*Gael.*, swift or nimble) tripped up Jean Armour at a wedding and gave him the chance to speak to the woman who was to be his wife and the abiding love of his life. Burns called one of 'The Twa Dogs' Luath after Cuchullin's hunting dog in Ossian's *Fingal*. Luath Press was established in 1981 in the heart of Burns country, and is now based a few steps up the road from Burns' first lodgings on Edinburgh's Royal Mile.

Luath offers you distinctive writing with a hint of unexpected pleasures.

Most bookshops in the UK, the US, Canada, Australia, New Zealand and parts of Europe either carry our books in stock or can order them for you. To order direct from us, please send a £sterling cheque, postal order, international money order or your credit card details (number, address of cardholder and expiry date) to us at the address below. Please add post and packing as follows: UK – £1.00 per delivery address; overseas surface mail – £2.50 per delivery address; overseas airmail – £3.50 for the first book to each delivery address, plus £1.00 for each additional book by airmail to the same address. If your order is a gift, we will happily enclose your card or message at no extra charge.

ILLUSTRATION: IAN KELLAS

Luath Press Limited
543/2 Castlehill
The Royal Mile
Edinburgh EH1 2ND
Scotland
Telephone: 0131 225 4326 (24 hours)
Fax: 0131 225 4324
email: sales@luath.co.uk
Website: www.luath.co.uk